MARY BERRY COOKS

MARY BERRY COOKS

Mary Berry

BOOKS

This book is published to accompany the television series entitled *Mary Berry Cooks*, first broadcast on BBC Two in 2014.

This Edition published 2014 for Index Books

Executive Producers: Anna Beattie, Richard Bowron
Series Director: Scott Tankard
Producer: Sophie Lloyd
Unit Manager: Nina Richards

3 5 7 9 10 8 6 4 2

Published in 2014 by BBC Books, an imprint of Ebury Publishing.
A Random House Group Company.

Photography by Georgia Glynn Smith
with the exception of pages 40 and 216 by Noel Murphy

Mary Berry has asserted her right to be identified as the author of this
Work in accordance with the Copyright, Designs and Patents Act 1988

The Random House Group Limited Reg. No. 954009

Addresses for companies within the Random House Group can be found
at www.randomhouse.co.uk

A CIP catalogue record for this book is available from the British Library.

ISBN: 978 1 849 90663 0

The Random House Group Limited supports the Forest Stewardship
Council® (FSC®), the leading international forest-certification
organisation. Our books carrying the FSC label are printed on FSC®-
certified paper. FSC is the only forest-certification
scheme supported by the leading environmental organisations,
including Greenpeace. Our paper procurement policy can be found
at www.randomhouse.co.uk/environment

Printed and bound in Germany by Mohn Media GmbH
Colour origination by AltaImage, London

To buy books by your favourite authors and register for offers visit
www.randomhouse.co.uk

CONTENTS

INTRODUCTION

I cannot tell you how thrilled I am to be able to pass on my knowledge, through *Mary Berry Cooks*, not just on baking but on how to entertain family and friends through my love of good food.

No matter what I am cooking, I want it to be as simple and as fuss-free as possible. Everything must be absolutely delicious, of course, but whether you are entertaining a handful of close friends, cooking a family meal, or creating a buffet party for a summer's day, the last thing you need is stress in the kitchen. This is why my dishes always contain elements that can be made in advance, or frozen to avoid any last-minute hassle.

As a working mother many years ago, it was essential that I had home-cooked dishes for my children when I finished work, and even now that they are older, I have kept the habit of making as much as I can in advance. In fact, over the past few years I have found myself busier than ever, so to come home and have a supper ready to defrost from the freezer is still a godsend!

It has been years since I presented my very own programme, but I was delighted to have the opportunity in *Mary Berry Cooks* to show how to entertain in a simple, stress-free way. This book includes all the recipes from the series, along with my wealth of experience on how to cook for special occasions without being a slave to the stove – my mantra is 'prepare ahead at all times' and this book will give you all the tools you need. There are plenty of tips on what you can and can't freeze ahead of time, as well as advice on how to present your dishes for maximum impact.

I love parties – who doesn't? – and several times a year we open the gardens for the National Garden Scheme charity, and host church plant sales in the garden. For these, I always provide tea, coffee, cakes and sandwiches, and have got calculating how much to serve each time down to a fine art!

As you can imagine, I have had many family celebrations over the years, too, as my children have grown up, married, and had children of their own – so of course there have been numerous birthday parties, Christmas celebrations, and many other excuses for a jolly good time. I could never bring myself to buy ready-made party foods (although there is nothing wrong with cheating by using ready-made pastry and buying in some spare crisps and nibbles), so over the years, I have developed recipes that are easy to make, but guaranteed to please, and will allow you to cater for almost any occasion.

In this collection, I have included some of my tried and trusted favourites, such as my Roast Fillet of Beef with Roasted Garlic and Mustard Cream (page 184), and Salmon Tranches with Herb Sauce, Quail's Eggs and Asparagus (page 156) – both impressive contributions to a summer buffet, but effortless to prepare ahead.

For drinks parties, I like to serve light, delicious canapés and have developed some lovely new ideas for this book which are quick and easy for you to make and serve. My moreish Croque Monsieur Toasts (page 45), Smoked Salmon Skewers (page 54) and Cocktail Palmiers (page 44) are all deceptively easy to make, but are certain to delight your party guests.

And for those winter nights when you just want to invite a few friends round for an intimate supper, there are plenty of recipes for hearty casseroles, bakes, and a fabulous Spiced Garden Vegetable Casserole (page 134) for vegetarians, all of which can easily be scaled up for bigger gatherings.

Of course, what dinner party would be complete without the pudding? Dessert can often feel like an afterthought, or another added stress to an already busy kitchen, but even simple puddings can provide a spectacular finish to a meal. Try my favourite, Warm Chocolate Fondant Tart (page 266), which can be made and frozen well in advance. Or as the days get longer, a spectacular Summer Pudding Loaf (page 234), which uses the best that the British hedgerows have to offer.

Afternoon tea is once again on the rise, with more and more people discovering the joys of baking. So I couldn't go without including my classic recipes for Teatime Scones (page 301) and Orange Butterfly Cakes (page 280), but have also included some wonderful ideas for simple 'cut-and-come-again' loaves to share over a cup of tea with a few friends, tray bakes that are perfect for a cake sale, and beautiful layer cakes for that special occasion.

A chapter on my Kitchen Wisdom gives you the tips and tricks that I have developed over the years. While it is not intended to be comprehensive, I hope that some of my suggestions on stocking your larder, meal planning, and catering for crowds, will be useful for you too.

Throughout the book, I have included the menus from the television show, so you can see my favourite meals to cook for each occasion, before embarking on your own. But all the recipes are suitable for entertaining, so I do hope that you will have fun experimenting with courses and combinations to find your own favourites among this collection, and that you enjoy the recipes as much as we have enjoyed creating them!

Mary Berry

Mary's Kitchen Wisdom

IN MY LARDER

As you can imagine, I have a well-stocked larder full of ingredients to call on, which makes all the difference when you have to rustle up a last-minute dinner or want to make a whole new meal out of last night's leftovers. Here are some of the ingredients from the recipes in this book that I like to use and often have to hand, which would be a useful addition to your store cupboard too.

GRAINS, PASTA AND PULSES

CHICKPEAS

A nourishing, filling pulse that is full of protein and can be used to bulk out soups and stews or in couscous salads. Chickpeas are available dried or canned but I tend to opt for the latter for reasons of convenience as the dried variety needs lengthy soaking.

COUSCOUS

Couscous is a grain made from semolina. It is very convenient to have in the store cupboard as it needs no cooking; you simply soak it in boiling water (or you can steam it over boiling water) for 10 minutes to make it plump up and soften. Couscous has a mild flavour that is delicious as it is, but to boost it you can soak it in stock, or add lemon juice and other seasonings to the soaking liquid.

Traditionally served in Arabic countries to accompany tagines, couscous soaks up the juices from stews beautifully so makes a good starchy substitute for rice or potatoes.

Alternatively, it makes a great base for salads – add roasted vegetables, chopped mint and coriander, nuts, dried fruits, or pomegranate seeds to give lots of colour and texture.

Giant couscous is now available and is cooked and used in the same way.

LENTILS

Lentils are an inexpensive store cupboard ingredient and are a good source of protein. You can buy dried red, yellow, green and brown lentils, and they will keep for up to one year stored in an airtight container. Canned lentils are also available.

Red and yellow lentils

These lentils cook quickly and soon turn soft and pulpy. They are ideal for thickening stews and soups, and are the basis of many variations of Indian dhal.

Puy lentils

These grey-brown French lentils, which keep their round, firm shape when cooked, are considered to be the finest. They have a distinctive earthy flavour and are delicious

served as an accompaniment to sausages and grilled meats or in salads.

How to cook lentils

Lentils do not need soaking. Rinse them, then cook them in water or in stock as described in the recipe, boiling them for the first 5 minutes, then simmering them until cooked and tender, which can take anything from 10 minutes to an hour depending on the type and the age of the lentils. Salt will toughen lentils so season them at the end of cooking.

PASTA

Pasta is an ingredient I often turn to when I'm in need of a quick, easy supper so I make sure I always have a variety of shapes in my cupboard, as well as spaghetti and lasagne sheets.

RICE

Rice is such a versatile ingredient: it can form the basis of a meal in itself – as a risotto or a salad, for example, while long-grain, basmati and other types, such as wild rice, can bulk out a meal as an accompaniment. As well as long-grain rice, here are the types I always have to hand.

Arborio rice

This is the classic risotto rice from Piedmont in Northern Italy. The grains are short and quite plump; translucent at the edge with a hard core, which is what gives them their distinctive creamy exterior with the 'al dente' or slightly chalky middle.

Carnaroli is another premium risotto rice; it has slightly longer grains than arborio.

Basmati rice

This is a long-grain Indian rice. When cooked its grains are light and fluffy and as is to be expected, their delicate, aromatic flavour complements Asian dishes particularly well.

Camargue red rice

Cultivated in the Camargue region of France this reddish-brown rice takes between 20 and 30 minutes to cook and has a delicious nutty flavour and a slightly chewy texture. Serve it alongside grilled meats or use it to make rice salads.

How to cook rice

One of the easiest and most reliable methods of cooking rice is to cook it in double its volume of water. Measure out 85ml (3fl oz) rice per person in a measuring jug. Tip the rice into a saucepan then measure double the amount – 150ml (¼ pint) per person – of cold water, and pour on top of the rice with ½ tsp salt.

Bring the water to the boil, stir once, then cover the pan with a tight-fitting lid and reduce the heat to its lowest setting. Cook for 10 minutes before opening the lid. By this time the rice should be cooked and will have absorbed all the water, leaving the grains fluffy and tender. If not, return the lid and cook for a few more minutes until all the water is absorbed.

CANNED AND PRESERVED FOODS

ANCHOVIES

Related to the herring family, these tiny oily fish are filleted, salted in brine and canned or packed into jars. Their piquant flavour makes an excellent seasoning. Look for jars or cans of anchovies in olive oil or salt. If packed in salt they should be rinsed and patted dry before use. Cans and jars of anchovies will store well in the kitchen cupboard, but once opened should be decanted into a small airtight container, covered with olive oil and consumed within two days.

CAPERS

These are the flowering buds of the Mediterranean caper bush and are used to flavour sauces with their salty, sour taste. The buds are picked and preserved in salt or olive oil, or pickled in vinegar. Larger, sweeter caper berries are also available.

COCONUT MILK AND CREAM

Coconut milk is the liquid that is produced when coconut is grated (not to be confused with coconut juice or water, which is the liquid inside the coconut). It is sold in cans and generally separates – a thick, creamy layer forms above a runny liquid – so it should be stirred well before use. It is delicious in curries and soups. Once opened the milk needs to be kept in the fridge and used within a day or two, or decant it and freeze it for up to six months.

Coconut cream is a hard block of compressed coconut flesh that is very rich and creamy and has to be chopped or grated before being added to curries, sauces and sometimes cakes. It can be kept in the store cupboard or fridge for several months.

DRIED PORCINI MUSHROOMS

Porcini (also know as ceps), with their deep earthy flavour, are thought to be the finest of mushrooms but they are also one of the most expensive and are available fresh for only a few months of the year. Happily, dried porcini are readily available and are a brilliant store cupboard essential. They are simple to prepare – you simply soak them in warm water until soft – then they can be snipped into pieces and added to risottos, chicken, game and beef casseroles and sauces to give a strong mushroom flavour. Don't throw out the soaking water, it will have a lot of flavour too so add it to the dish you are cooking.

Dried wild mushrooms are also available and can be used in the same way but don't have the depth of flavour of porcini.

OLIVES

Olives are widely grown in Spain, Italy, France and Greece. They are considered an essential ingredient in these countries' cuisines so are a useful ingredient to add

a touch of sunshine to your cooking or simply as a delicious nibble with drinks.

Inedible raw, olives are brined before eating. Green olives are the unripe fruit, turning to brownish pink and then black as they ripen. Natural black olives are picked fresh, but the shiny black olives you can buy are often green olives that have been cured and treated to give the jet black colour.

Olives can often be marinated in olive oil with garlic, herbs, chillies or citrus rind. Often they are stuffed with pimento, rolled anchovies or whole blanched almonds.

Kalamata olives are purple, almond shaped olives grown in southern Greece. They have a distinctive fruity flavour and are usually sold brined. Manzanilla olives are small, succulent green Spanish olives.

TOMATOES

Canned tomatoes

An essential store cupboard ingredient used in bolognese sauces, stews and casseroles as they have a richer, more concentrated flavour than fresh tomatoes. Two types are available: whole, peeled plum as well as chopped. They are largely interchangeable but some people feel the whole tomatoes have a better flavour.

Passata

Made by cooking, then sieving tomatoes, passata is a thick but juicy pulp that is ideal as a base for pasta sauces, soups and stews. Available either smooth or chunky or with herbs and garlic added.

Sun-dried/sun-blushed tomatoes

Sun-dried tomatoes have had most of their moisture removed so they will keep for longer than fresh in the store cupboard. They have an intense, sweet flavour, a slightly chewy texture and have so many uses in cooking: add them to soups, stews and pasta sauces, or give savoury bakes a strong tomatoey flavour without adding too much extra moisture.

Sun-blushed or 'sun-ripened' tomatoes are plumper and sweeter than sun-dried tomatoes as they are only partly dried and are kept in olive oil to preserve them. They work well in salads and sandwiches.

Tomato purée

A thick paste made by cooking tomatoes for several hours, then straining them to remove the seeds. Keep a tube of purée in the fridge to add depth of flavour to bolognese sauces, pasta sauces, casseroles and risottos.

OILS, VINEGARS, SEASONINGS AND CONDIMENTS

GARLIC

In my view, no kitchen supply is complete without garlic.

Crushing garlic is the strongest way to use it: peel then cut in half and place on a chopping board with a little sea salt. Lay a large knife over the garlic and press down with the heel of your hand to crush, then scrape the blade back and forth over the garlic until finely crushed. A garlic crusher makes this job much simpler.

Garlic may also be chopped or sliced for a milder flavour – it is often used this way when stir-frying dishes. When frying garlic, never allow it to brown as this will mean it's burnt and bitter.

Whole cloves of garlic or indeed whole bulbs of garlic can be roasted or added to a dish to give a mild sweet flavour. When roasted squeeze the garlic paste from a bulb to give a deliciously mild sweet purée.

Store garlic in a cool, dry, airy place and it will last several weeks.

HARISSA PASTE

Made from ground chilli peppers (often smoked or dried) and garlic, this pungent red paste originated in North Africa where it is widely used in recipes. Recipes vary so it may contain coriander, caraway or cumin, and usually olive oil. It may also contain tomatoes, or even crushed rose petals.

Try adding harissa to salad dressings for a fiery rich flavour; spread it thinly over pizza doughs; stir it into tagines, soups and stews and marinades for lamb or chicken dishes; smother it over barbecue meats and fish before cooking; or stir it into crème fraîche or Greek yoghurt to make an instant dip.

Once opened, pour a thin layer of olive oil over the paste and store it in the fridge.

HONEY

This is really handy for both sweet and savoury dishes, though I actually find I use it more often in the latter – in tagines, curries and marinades, for example. Clear rather than cloudy honey is the more versatile for cooking – choose a neutral-flavoured variety, rather than a heavily scented one such as lavender, or the floral flavour will overpower your dish.

HORSERADISH

It can be hard to source fresh horseradish unless you grow you own, but jars of grated horseradish and creamed horseradish with oil, cream and vinegar added are useful to keep in the cupboard. Horseradish is a member of the mustard family so it is quite strong and hot – delicious with roast beef and smoked fish.

MUSTARD

The seeds of the mustard plant are cracked or bruised and mixed with salt, water or lemon juice to make this flavoursome condiment. Mustards vary in strength, so it is useful to stock the three basics: mellow, rich Dijon mustard, which is excellent in dressings or to smear on bread to make sandwiches; coarse grain mustards, delicious in marinades and dressings; and hot, pungent English Mustard which is perfect to serve with roast beef, hams and gammon, either on the plate or in sandwiches. Sweeter American mustard is also popular to serve with burgers or hot dogs.

SESAME OIL

Derived from sesame seeds, the oil is used to flavour Asian dishes, particularly Chinese food. It has quite a strong flavour so just a few drops added at the end of the cooking will give a delicious nuttiness to the dish, or you can stir-fry in it directly for a very intense flavour.

SOY SAUCE

Made from fermented soy beans, water and barley or wheat, soy sauce is used in Asian cooking as a seasoning. Light soy sauce is thin and salty, while dark soy sauce is richer and slightly thicker. Low-salt options are also available. Use it as you would salt and pepper in any savoury dish to give a little more depth of flavour than usual – it can also be used as a condiment in the same way as vinegar.

VINEGAR

Vinegars are a really useful store cupboard ingredient – vital for vinaigrettes and dressings but also handy for marinades, sweet-and-sour sauces, pickles and chutneys and as a condiment. I like to keep at least five or six different types in my cupboard as they are each so unique.

Those listed here are the ones I would have as a minimum, however there is also a wide range of herb and spice vinegars, such as chilli, tarragon or raspberry vinegars available and I love experimenting with these.

Balsamic Vinegar

The most authentic type of balsamic vinegar is made from grape must (juice) that is simmered until very concentrated and then left to ferment for a minimum of 12 years in wooden barrels. The fermentation imparts unique flavours, and during the process the vinegar becomes thick, dark and syrupy.

This high-quality vinegar comes from Modena, in the Emilia Romagna region of Italy. Look for the word 'tradizionale' for the best quality. It will be expensive but you need only use it in very small quantities and so will last you a long time. Alternatively, a cheaper option is 'aceto balsamico di Modena'. This has not been aged for so long, but is made using the same principle.

Be wary of other products masquerading as 'balsamic vinegar'. These are most likely cheap imitations that have caramel added to colour them.

Balsamic glaze

This rich and sticky balsamic vinegar reduction has a sweet and slightly sour flavour, and is delicious drizzled over salads or used to make a quick sauce.

Using balsamic vinegar

Use the best-quality 'tradizionale' balsamic where you will really appreciate its unique flavour. For an amazingly simple dessert, try it drizzled over sliced strawberries or good-quality vanilla ice cream. Drop a little into a small bowl of extra virgin olive oil and serve it with chunks of crusty bread for dipping.

Use less expensive 'aceto balsamico di Modena' in cooking. Add a drizzle to the pan juices of steaks, pork chops, duck or chicken breasts, or stir it into pasta dishes, risottos and marinades.

For salads, add just a few drops of balsamic to any oil and vinegar dressing to give it a rich flavour.

Malt vinegar

Made from fermenting barley and traditionally used to sprinkle over fish and chips or used in preserves.

Red and white wine vinegar

Made by fermenting red or white wines, their tangy and rich flavours are ideal to use in salad dressings. I use white wine vinegar for almost everything.

Rice wine vinegar

A mild-flavoured vinegar mainly used in Chinese cookery. It pairs well with such flavours such as soy and sesame oil and is often used to make simple marinades.

Sherry and cider vinegar

Milder than wine vinegars, and with sweeter flavours, these are particularly good for dressings due to their unique flavours.

FRESH HERBS

BASIL

The soft, shiny green leaves of this Mediterranean herb are the essential ingredient in pesto and are widely used in many Italian dishes. Basil is a very delicate herb and retains more flavour if torn rather than chopped with a knife. Similarly, always add basil at the end of cooking as prolonged heat will destroy its flavour.

Keep growing pots of basil fresh by keeping them on a sunny windowsill and always water from the base of the pot. Pick off wilted leaves, and the plant should grow for several weeks.

Basil should not be kept in the fridge as the leaves will turn black.

CORIANDER

Coriander is a tender, green leafy herb with a distinctive citrus flavour. It is widely used in Asian and Mexican dishes. Heat diminishes the flavour of coriander so add it to hot dishes at the last moment or use it raw. Add chopped or whole leaves to curries, salsas, guacamole and salads.

Store packets of coriander in the door of the fridge for 2-3 days only – it will wilt very quickly and does not freeze or dry well.

DILL

A wonderful herb to have in stock if you are cooking with fish as the flavours marry beautifully.

FENNEL

The feathery leaves – or fronds – of the fennel bulb have a pronounced aniseed flavour. It belongs to the same family as dill, and like that herb, too, fennel is a perfect partner to fish. Try barbecuing or cooking fish on top of the herb for a gentle fragrance.

Fennel seeds are sweet and liquorice-flavoured. They are commonly sprinkled on top of bread rolls for a unique flavour or added to Italian salamis.

LEMONGRASS

A woody stalk, composed of tightly packed leaves, this is one of the most distinctive flavourings in many dishes from Southeast Asia, particularly Thailand and Vietnam.

Crush the bulbous base of the stalk with the end of a rolling pin to release its aromatic juices or slice, then add to curries and soups.

The flavour is excellent in savoury dishes, paired with fish, prawns and chicken, but lemongrass can also be used to impart flavour to sweet syrups for fruit cocktails and to flavour lemonade, custards and cocktails. Lemongrass should be removed before serving.

Store it wrapped in damp kitchen paper in the fridge for up to two weeks.

Dried lemongrass is also available but is less fragrant – it should be soaked in water before use.

MINT

There are many varieties of this refreshing herb available, each with its own subtle flavour and appearance.

Spearmint has pointed, serrated-edged leaves and is the most commonly used in cooking as it has an excellent flavour. Peppermint has longer, darker leaves and a stronger flavour, which is best used in confectionery. Apple mint leaves are rounder and furrier, and it has a sweeter, fruitier flavour so is often used in refreshing summer drinks.

Pluck the leaves from the stem then chop or shred them finely.

Keep packs of mint in the door of the fridge for up to three days.

PARSLEY

This is one of the most versatile herbs, and the one I use the most as the flavour complements so many different meats and vegetables and types of cuisine.

There are two types available: curly and flat-leaf. Curly has the milder flavour. Flat-leaf is darker and has a more robust flavour that stands up to cooking, while curly is often used for garnishing.

The two are interchangeable, however, so I often don't specify a type in my recipes – just use whichever you prefer.

I add parsley to dressings, sauces, pasta dishes and stuffings, and also as a garnish.

OREGANO & MARJORAM

Oregano grows wild in southern Europe and the Mediterranean. Marjoram is from the same herb family and is sometimes used interchangeably. Often used in Italian and Greek dishes, they have a great affinity to lamb, tomatoes, vegetables and eggs.

Fresh oregano or marjoram will last for one week in the fridge, but because of its high oil content will also dry well if left in a warm room for a few days.

ROSEMARY

This is a fragrant, versatile herb that is best used fresh. Take leaves off the stem and chop finely, or use branches of rosemary to add flavour to your roasts.

SAGE

A very easy herb to grow all year round, the soft velvety leaves have a slightly musky scent. Sage can withstand prolonged cooking without loss of flavour and it also dries well. The flavour goes well with pork and chicken, and it is often used in sausages, roasts and stuffings.

Whole leaves can be fried in butter or oil until crisp and then scattered over pasta, tortellini or gnocchi. Keep packs of sage

leaves in the door of the fridge for 2–3 days and discard when the leaves turn black. To dry your own, simply hang it in a cool place until dried – it takes about two weeks.

TARRAGON

Fresh French tarragon is a long, slender green herb with an intense, almost aniseed flavour with hints of vanilla. Often used in French cooking, it is a perfect match for chicken and can also be used to flavour oils and vinegars.

Russian tarragon has very fine, thin leaves. It is often sold as a tarragon plant, but tastes like grass!

Store fresh tarragon wrapped in damp kitchen paper in the fridge for a maximum of 3–4 days.

THYME

This shrubby herb has tiny greyish-green leaves full of an intense aromatic oil that gives a real depth of flavour to meaty casseroles, stews and roasted vegetables. Like sage, it stands up well to long cooking times, imparting its flavour slowly and gently.

Sprigs of thyme can be added whole to dishes, or the leaves can be pulled off and chopped and rubbed over meat and chicken before grilling or barbecuing.

There are many varieties of thyme with which to experiment; try the citrus notes of lemon thyme for a change.

CARDAMOM

There are two types of cardamom – green and black. Both are small pods that contain clusters of small black seeds. Green cardamom is the more commonly available – you're unlikely to be able to find black cardamom in the supermarket – and it is the one I use. You can use both the whole pods or crack them open and use the seeds, but note that whole pods are not supposed to be eaten. To get most of the flavour out of the pods, bruise them with a rolling pin before adding to the pan. Seeds are often sold separately by Indian grocers, but you can also take the seeds out of the pods yourself.

Ground cardamom is also available but doesn't have the same aromas and fragrance as the whole spice.

CHILLI

I know that not everyone likes a lot of heat in their food, but if you use chillies judiciously, they can add a gentle warmth to your dishes that really is essential in certain cuisines.

The pith and seeds are the most potent parts of a chilli, so remove them for a milder heat. Cut the chillies in half, lengthways, remove the seeds and pith then slice or dice as required.

If you burn your mouth with chilli, drinking water will do no good because the spicy part – capsaicin – is not soluble in water. Drink milk or yoghurt, or eat ice cream or even peanut butter.

Below is a guide to the chillies I use most frequently.

Cayenne

Made from ground chillies, this is a hot and fiery spice that is used to add spicy heat. Drying a chilli increases its potency, so cayenne should be used sparingly as it really is strong and you can always add more but you can't take it away! A pinch of cayenne adds a hint of spice when dusted over cheese biscuits, prawn cocktails or egg mayonnaise.

Dried chilli flakes

Useful to keep in the spice cupboard to use when you don't have fresh. They are good to add to salsas or sprinkled into pastries and scones to give an extra hint of flavour, though again, use with caution as they are surprisingly hot!

Jalepeño chilli peppers

These are the most popular and widely available chillies that you will find in the supermarket. Either red or green, they are bullet-shaped with a soft, smooth skin and range from medium to pretty hot. If you like a really hot chilli use tiny bird's eye chillies, which have a fruity, pungent heat.

How to prepare fresh chillies

It is best to use rubber gloves when preparing chillies, as the juice is very strong and easily absorbed by the skin, causing a burning sensation.

Always wash your hands thoroughly with soap and water after preparing chillies, and never touch your eyes or other sensitive areas when handling chillies, as the capsaicin can really burn.

CORIANDER

Very different to the flavour of the fresh herb, the seeds of the coriander plant have a delicious warm, nutty, lemony or orangey citrus flavour when crushed.

Coriander is available to buy as whole seeds or ground, but as with most spices the whole seed is the more potent and for a stronger flavour, it's better to toast then grind the whole spice yourself. Toasting coriander seeds in a dry frying pan will bring out their nuttiness.

Coriander seeds are widely used in curries, often partnered with cumin seeds.

CUMIN

Cumin seeds are tiny, oval, brown-ridged seeds with a very distinctive, sweetish aroma widely used to season curries, and in Indian, Middle Eastern and Mexican cuisines. You can dry fry them to intensify their flavour but it's not essential. Also available ground.

FIVE-SPICE POWDER

A Chinese blend of five flavours – salty, sour, bitter, pungent and sweet, hence its name. It is a mixture of ground star anise, fennel, cloves, cinnamon and Sichuan pepper. I use it in stir-fries or add it to barbecue sauces and marinades.

GINGER

A small knobbly root (a rhizome), ginger has an unusual flavour – it adds freshness yet also spicy warmth, so is widely used in curries, stir-fries, chutneys, salsas and sauces.

Peel ginger with a potato peeler and finely shred, chop or grate the fibrous flesh before use. Store fresh ginger in the salad drawer of the fridge where it will last a couple of weeks, or freeze it and grate it straight from the freezer.

Don't be tempted to use fresh ginger in cakes and biscuits as the flavour becomes bitter. Dried, powdered ginger is more suitable for use in baking.

NUTMEG

Nutmeg has a warm, sweet, nutty flavour, and is used in a variety of cooking contexts. Although ground nutmeg is available, it is best to buy whole nutmeg kernels and grate them as needed; as with all spices the flavour is much stronger.

Nutmeg is a lovely complement to dairy products and is delicious sprinkled over a creamy rice pudding or a pumpkin pie, while a grating added to béchamel sauce or bread sauce really improves the flavour. Yet there are other classic flavour pairings – it is wonderful sprinkled over wilted buttered

spinach, roasted pumpkin, or fresh pasta with hot butter. It is also widely used in cakes and desserts, and in mulled wine.

PAPRIKA

Like cayenne pepper, paprika is made by grinding dried red peppers or chillies. It is a very popular spice in Hungary, Spain (where it is known as *pimentón*) and Portugal, and is used to give goulash and chorizo sausages their characteristic flavours. Although generally milder than cayenne, paprika's strength does vary; some are sweet, some hot and some medium, so always check the label.

Smoked paprika is made from peppers that have been smoked first and the flavour is reminiscent of smoky bacon. Again check the label for sweet or hot varieties.

SESAME SEEDS

The tiny, cream seeds of the sesame plant have a subtle, nutty flavour and are delicious sprinkled over salads, added to bread mixes or sprinkled over stir-fries and Chinese dishes. Tahini is a sesame-seed paste, used to flavour houmous and the Middle Eastern sweet known as halva.

Sesame seeds can be dry-fried in a frying pan to give a more distinctive nutty flavour. Fry gently and carefully as they burn easily.

BAKING INGREDIENTS

BAKING POWDER

Baking powder is used to give lightness to baked recipes such as scones, cakes, pastries and sometimes batter, as well as to make certain mixtures rise. It is a combination of acidic cream of tartar and mild alkaline bicarbonate of soda. Always check the use-by date as baking powder will lose its potency when past its best, and store it in an airtight container as moisture will also reduce its efficiency.

How to make your own baking powder
If you find you have run out of baking powder you can make your own.

To make the equivalent of one teaspoon of baking powder, mix half a teaspoon of cream of tartar with a quarter of a teaspoon of bicarbonate of soda (sometimes called baking soda).

CRYSTALLISED ROSE PETALS

These have a delicate, perfumed flavour and are delicious sprinkled over icing on cupcakes or added to biscuits, such as in my Rose Petal Biscuits on page 299. Crystallised violets are also available and can be used in the same way.

FLOUR

Although there are a range of flours available, for the cakes and other teatime bakes in this book there are really only two types of flour you will need: plain and self-raising.

For cakes or bakes that need a rise, plain flour needs to be used in conjunction with a raising agent. Self-raising flour is simply flour that has the baking powder already incorporated, although as you will see, sometimes it is also used with a raising agent to give it a little extra lift.

To turn plain flour into self-raising flour, add 2–3 teaspoons of baking powder to every 200g (7oz) of plain flour.

FREEZE-DRIED STRAWBERRY AND RASPBERRY PIECES

These tiny pieces of freeze-dried fruits have a very concentrated flavour so a little goes a long way. Scatter them into muesli and yoghurt for breakfast; stir into cake mixtures or grind to a powder and use in butter icings, meringues and cake mixtures.

GOLDEN SYRUP

I find this a useful item to have in the cupboard as it's an essential ingredient in my flapjack recipes, which are such a quick and easy bake to whip up, while children love it poured over waffles or pancakes for pudding.

MAPLE SYRUP

Made from the sap of red maple or black maple trees and mainly harvested in Canada, this a sweet syrup, which has a unique flavour. It is traditionally served poured over American pancakes – often with bacon too – but is delicious drizzled over ice cream or added to cakes and icings, milkshakes and marinades. It can be used instead of golden syrup in some recipes but its thinner consistency may affect the end result.

SUGAR

Given how frequently I bake, I keep a wide range of sugar varieties in my cupboard as different sugars serve different purposes. Below is a list of the ones I think are absolutely essential if you're going to be baking regularly and the ones that are in my cupboard without fail, but I've made a note of those that are really for keen bakers and not necessarily ones that I use every day.

As a general rule, I prefer to use unrefined sugars. Keep unrefined sugars in a container with a lid. It doesn't have to be airtight as the sugar will keep moist if it can absorb moisture from the air. If your sugar has become hard, put a slice of bread in the container overnight, or warm the sugar in the microwave for just a second or two before use – take care to do this in very short bursts or it will burn.

Caster sugar

I stock two different types of caster sugar: refined white, which is the best for meringues; and unrefined caster sugar, which I prefer to use for sponge cakes (though this is a personal choice and refined caster sugar serves exactly the same purpose).

Demerara sugar

This is a rich, golden-brown sugar with large crunchy crystals and a creamy toffee flavour. It is made from pressed sugar cane, which is then steamed until the juice produces a thick cane syrup. This is then dehydrated to form large brown crystals. It gives a delicious crunch when sprinkled on top of cakes and crumbles, and is the perfect sugar to use in coffee as it lends the coffee a gentle caramel flavour.

Icing sugar

I use white icing sugar for most cakes, but also like unrefined icing sugar, which has a pale golden colour and a slight caramel flavour. It is ideal if you're making a caramel-flavoured buttercream.

Fondant icing sugar

This is essentially icing sugar mixed with dried glucose syrup. It is used to make a stiff fondant icing which can be rolled out to cover cakes, or to make a thick, glossy pouring icing that will set on top of cupcakes or fondant fancies. This is one for keen bakers as it takes a bit more skill to master how to use it.

Muscovado sugar

Made from unrefined sugar cane, muscovado sugar is moist and has a distinctive caramel flavour. There are three types, which vary according to the amount of molasses (the residual liquid produced during the sugar-making process) they contain. Light muscovado sugar is delicious in cakes and biscuits, and gives a good colour as well as flavour. Dark muscovado sugar has an even stronger, more treacley flavour and is perfect for making dark rich fruit cakes and gingerbreads. Molasses sugar is even richer and stickier with a deep flavour that is ideal to make barbecue sauces.

Make sure you are buying unrefined sugar rather than simply 'brown sugars', which are often refined white sugars coated in molasses to colour them.

VANILLA

Vanilla pods are the long, black, dried seed pods of a climbing orchid from Madagascar. They add a delicate flavour to many desserts. Try infusing whole vanilla pods in warm milk to make a deliciously scented custard or ice cream. For a more pronounced flavour, cut the pods in half lengthways and, using the tip of a knife, scrape out the black seed paste and add this to dessert mixtures. When you have used the pods, dry them and place in a jar of caster sugar where they will gently scent the sugar to use in cakes and biscuits.

Vanilla essence

An inexpensive synthetic product that is best avoided.

Vanilla extract

The extract is 'vanillin', which is what gives vanilla its wonderful flavour. As it is taken from the natural source it is far more expensive than essence but a little goes a long way – just a little will scent a cake mixture or custard.

THE FREEZER

I believe the freezer is one of the home cook's best friends, and it would certainly have been difficult for me to cope with feeding a family or entertaining if I could not have prepared a number of recipes in advance, freezing them until needed. I also hate waste, so I try to freeze anything left over instead of leaving it in the fridge hoping it will be used up quickly.

The trick to using your freezer wisely is to keep a note of everything you have in there. I keep mine as a list stuck on the inside of my kitchen cupboard. Look at your list before you make a meal and cross items off when they have been eaten.

WHAT YOU CAN FREEZE

Main courses

I find it invaluable to freeze meals for supper or dinner parties, and will often double up a recipe to make one dish for supper and one for another time. Most cooked dishes are best frozen for no longer than 3 months so they retain their original flavour.

Vegetables

They do taste better fresh, but vegetables can be a useful thing to have in the freezer. Most vegetables need to be blanched before freezing as this helps to retain their colour, texture, flavour and the vitamins within them. Plunge them into boiling water and cook for 1–3 minutes, then immediately drain and plunge into ice-cold water. Certain watery vegetables, such as cucumber, endives, lettuce, radishes and artichokes, cannot be frozen. Tomatoes can be frozen but are only suitable to add to casseroles as they become very watery.

Fruit

Most freeze well and make an excellent stand-by dessert. Apples, rhubarb, plums, peaches, cherries and gooseberries are best stewed with a little sugar. Soft fruits such as strawberries or peaches are best turned into purées as the whole frozen fruit will turn mushy when you defrost them. Smaller fruits like raspberries, blackberries, blackcurrants and redcurrants can be frozen whole.

Ginger

If you have some left over, freeze the whole root and grate from frozen. If peeled, wrap in clingfilm before freezing; if it still has its skin freeze it as it is.

Chilli

Chop whole chillies then freeze – you can add the chopped chilli directly from the freezer to your dish; it will defrost very quickly.

Cakes and puddings

Anything with delicate icing or decoration (such as piped cupcakes) should be open-frozen so that it is not damaged when wrapped or packaged. To open freeze, spread the items out on a tray and place in the freezer. When they are completely frozen, they can be packed in containers or bags without damaging the shape.

Biscuit and pastry dough

Biscuit dough can be frozen in a log shape, ready to be defrosted in the fridge then sliced and baked. Pastry cases can be frozen unbaked or baked blind ready to fill. Uncooked pastry freezes perfectly for up to 3 months.

Milk, cream and butter

It is useful to keep milk in the freezer; in emergencies it can be defrosted in a sink of cold water. The milk and fat will separate, but will homogenise again when shaken. Single cream and yoghurt do not freeze, but double and clotted cream do freeze as they have a higher fat content. Freeze cream for up to 3 months only. Butter and hard cheese (ideally grated so it is ready to use) are also useful to keep in the freezer – again for only 3 months. Buttercream icing does freeze well, but use after 3 months or the flavour will deteriorate.

Eggs

Whole eggs do not freeze well, so do not add them to a fish pie if you are freezing it. Egg whites can be frozen in small containers (make sure you label how many you have frozen) and are ideal for meringues. Egg yolks can also be frozen in small containers to enrich sauces or omelettes at a later date.

Wine

Don't let a drop of wine go to waste! Freeze it in ice cube trays ready to add to sauces. When frozen decant into small bags to store.

Jars of sauces

If you have half a jar of pasta sauce, roasted red peppers or pesto left over decant into containers and freeze. Passata and chopped tomatoes also freeze well if you have some spare.

WHAT YOU CAN'T FREEZE

Sugar paste and royal icing

This will become sticky when defrosted.

Salad ingredients

Ingredients like cucumber and lettuce contain too much water to freeze well.

Fresh basil, coriander and dill

It is better to make herbs into pesto or herb butters and freeze that instead.

Potatoes

If you are making a cottage pie or fish pie with mashed potato, add less milk and more butter to the potato or it will become watery when defrosted.

KNOW-HOW

- Cool foods after cooking or blanching before freezing.

- Exclude as much air as possible from packaged foods to prevent them drying out, and use the correct-sized container if possible.

- Keep washed cartons from ready-made foods. I wash out and keep ice cream and soup cartons that have tight-fitting lids as these are so useful for freezing portions of food.

- Wrap foods in foil first, then in waxed paper or a freezer bag.

- Always date and label the packages, and add cooking/reheating instructions too.

- Organise the shelves. Try to keep the same sorts of foods together in sections of your freezer. Keep vegetables in one drawer, desserts and cakes in another and so on. And keep a good rotation of stock, using up the oldest foods first. Keep all the small ingredients that will easily get lost in one area of the fridge (e.g. chillies, sausages, fresh herbs, cubes of stock or wine).

DEFROSTING

- If possible always defrost foods in the fridge for best results, or use the defrost setting on the microwave.

- You can defrost casseroles or soups on the hob, but stir thoroughly during defrosting to ensure they're heated through evenly.

- Meat, fish and poultry must reach boiling point for 10 minutes in the centre (3–4 minutes in the microwave) to ensure they are cooked thoroughly.

- Vegetables can be cooked from frozen.

- Some meals can be cooked from frozen: increase the cooking time in the recipe by half again and ensure the centre of the food has reached boiling point for at least 10 minutes before serving.

- If defrosting in the microwave, ensure food is of even thickness or it will cook unevenly.

MENU PLANNING

Whether you are planning a small dinner party, a Sunday lunch, a barbecue or a grand celebration, it is essential to plan not just the menu, but the time running up to the event too. While it might sound like a bore, a little forward planning and preparation can really help you to relax and enjoy the party on the day. This is why I have given you 'prepare ahead' instructions for as many recipes as possible in this book – they should help your events run smoothly with little or no last-minute worries.

CHOOSING YOUR DISHES

I usually start to plan my menus around the main course, thinking about how many people I will be serving and which ingredients are at their best at that time of year. In the winter, I might choose a casserole or a roast, while in summer, I am more likely to cook fish or chicken or serve cold cuts. To give people lots of choice, I try to serve at least two seasonal vegetables along with potatoes, rice or pasta.

I then choose the starter and pudding. It is important to have a mix of colours, textures and flavours in a menu, so if you have a pastry tartlet to start, you are unlikely to want a pastry dessert too, and if you have fish as a main course, avoid serving shellfish to start. Similarly, make sure you don't have too much cream in each course as this will start to feel very heavy (as well as not being good for your health!), and have a mixture of hot and cold dishes, some of which you can prepare in advance.

If feeding a crowd, I like to serve two desserts – one rich and chocolatey; one fruity. This needn't be very time consuming, as one or both can be prepared in advance.

PRESENTATION

It is always lovely – for you and for your guests – to make your room look a little bit special when entertaining. But making your table look inviting doesn't need to be hard work.

I like to arrange seasonal flowers in low containers on the table. Sometimes just a few blossoms in egg cups or pretty teacups placed down the centre of the table can look beautiful.

It is a good idea to arrange items for a buffet table in the order that they will be collected, so plates first, followed by the food – starter, mains, salads and desserts – followed by napkins and cutlery.

If you don't have enough glasses, you can usually hire extras on a return basis from supermarkets or wine merchants – or why not make little labels to tie around the stems, so that everybody keeps hold of their one glass for the evening?

HOW MUCH TO COOK

Over the years, I have been fortunate enough to have given many large parties at home and in the garden, and I have learned that the more people you have, the less they seem to eat!

Most people cook far more than they need to, and I always feel that it is a shame to be so wasteful. So below is a rough quantities calculator that I use to work out recipes for my events.

Of course, quantities will vary slightly depending on your guests (I always find teenagers have a huge appetite!), the time of day and the type of party you are hosting.

SAVOURY DISHES, PER PERSON:

Joint with bone: 175–225g (6–8oz)

Joint without bone: 100–175g (4–6oz)

Meat for casseroles: 175g (6oz)

Pasta, uncooked: 75–100g (3–4oz)

Rice, uncooked: 40–50g (1½–2oz)

Salmon: 100–125g (4–4½oz)

Soup: 600ml (1 pint) will serve 3 people

Fillet steak: 150g (5oz)

Other steaks: 175–200g (6–7 oz)

SWEET DISHES, PER PERSON:

Cakes: a 20cm (8in) sponge will feed 6

Meringues: 1 egg white and 50g (2oz) caster sugar will make about 5 small meringues

Soft fruits: 75–100g (3–4oz)

Cream to accompany desserts: 600ml (1 pint) per 12 portions

NIBBLES, PER PERSON:

Crisps: 25g (1oz)

Salted nuts: 15g (½oz)

SANDWICHES AND BREAD:

1 loaf, medium cut, makes 10 rounds of sandwiches

100g (4oz) butter is enough for 1 large sandwich loaf or 12 bread rolls

1 long baguette cuts into 20 slices

DRINKS:

Champagne: 1 bottle (75cl) will serve 6 full glasses (8 if pouring smaller measures)

Wine: 1 bottle (75cl) will serve 6 glasses

Soft drinks and mixers: 1 bottle (1 litre) will serve 6 glasses

Milk for coffee: allow 900ml (1½ pints) per 20 cups

Milk for tea: allow 600ml (1 pint) per 20 cups

Quick Bites and Canapés

QUICK BITES *and* CANAPÉS

Whenever we have something to celebrate I throw a drinks party with lots of savoury bites to eat. Whether it is a Christmas or New Year's gathering, a birthday or anniversary, or just a simple celebration of a family achievement or event, there is nothing nicer than getting lots of friends and family around for a couple of hours to raise a glass or two.

If having a drinks party sounds like a lot of work, believe me when I tell you that it has been my mission over the years to find quick and easy canapés that can be made ahead and have no last-minute preparation, yet will always look stylish and appealing when served.

Don't be shy about relying on certain ready-made products to help save you time. There's absolutely no shame in this, particularly as you can buy some really excellent-quality, tasty versions of certain ingredients. A packet of ready-rolled puff pastry can be turned into savoury Cocktail Palmiers (page 44) or Tiny Pesto Tartlets (page 57) in minutes, and a pack of ready-to-bake dough balls are the perfect bite-sized base for a rich goat's cheese topping (page 46).

A fresh chunk of tuna can be cut into cubes, marinated ahead of time then fried in seconds to be served on little cocktail sticks (page 51), while rare roast beef is rolled up around cream cheese and tarragon for deceptively smart treats (page 43). The simplest idea is a tiny stack of three delicate sandwiches on a cocktail stick (page 56). They can be made ahead, are easy to hold when you have a drink in one hand and are sophisticated enough to serve to adults, while the simple flavours will appeal to children too.

BEEF, TARRAGON AND *Horseradish* ROULADES

MAKES ABOUT
40 ROLLS

PREPARE AHEAD
Slice the beef then reassemble tightly to make it look like one piece again, then cover tightly in clingfilm. This will stop the beef oxidising and going brown. You can then assemble the rolls an hour or two ahead.

500g (1lb 2oz) piece of beef fillet, cut from the centre of the fillet

1 tablespoon sunflower oil

200g/7oz full-fat cream cheese

3 tablespoons creamed horseradish

a small bunch of tarragon

salt and freshly ground black pepper

These luxurious little roulades are impressive yet so easy to make. Beef fillet is expensive, but it has the wow factor for a special occasion – the melting texture and flavour are unrivalled. Best of all, the rolls can be completed a couple of hours before serving.

1 Let the beef come to room temperature 30 minutes before cooking. Pat dry and season with salt and black pepper.

2 Preheat the oven to 220°C/200°C fan/Gas 7. Heat the oil in a heavy-based frying pan and when hot, fry the beef, until all the sides are browned. Place the beef in a roasting tin and roast for 20 minutes for rare beef, a little less if it is a slim joint. Cover with foil and leave to cool. Chill in the fridge until firmed up and easy to slice.

3 When the beef is cold, use a sharp knife to cut it into slices, as thinly as you can.

4 Mix the cream cheese with the horseradish, then place in a small plastic piping bag and snip off the end to give a hole about 1cm across. Pipe the mixture over one end of each slice of beef. Alternatively, simply spread each slice of beef with a little of the mixture. Add a couple of tarragon leaves to each one then roll up tightly and cut the rolls in half. Stand them cut-side down on a serving tray and cover with clingfilm until ready to serve – ideally within a couple of hours; any longer and the beef may start to lose its lovely colour.

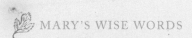 MARY'S WISE WORDS

To make just a few beef rolls, buy cooked, rare, sliced beef from the supermarket. Or if making a very large quantity why not buy ready-sliced pastrami and use in the same way?

Don't cook the fillet of beef until well done as it will not be as tender to eat and will not be such an appealing colour.

COCKTAIL *Palmiers*

MAKES 48 PALMIERS

FREEZE

Prepare and slice the uncooked
pastries then freeze on baking
trays until firm, then you
can pack them in a freezer
container and take out a few
when needed. Just bake in a
preheated oven for about
12 minutes or until brown
and crisp.

1 x 320g pack ready-rolled
puff pastry

1 tablespoon yeast extract

1 tablespoon olive tapenade

Ready-rolled puff pastry is one of the cook's greatest friends. There are such good versions to buy now that there's really no need to worry about making your own pastry, particularly for something like a canapé. These buttery, savoury little French pastries take full advantage of the time-saving benefits of ready-rolled pastry, and they are ideal for big parties as they can be prepared in large quantities.

1 You will need 2–3 baking trays. Preheat the oven to 220°C/200°C fan/Gas 7.

2 Unroll the pastry and cut it into eight strips, each about 5cm (2in) wide. Spread four strips thinly with the yeast extract, and the other four with the tapenade.

3 Roll up each piece of pastry tightly from one long side until it reaches the centre, then roll up the other side to meet it. Place the pastry rolls on a tray in the freezer for 10 minutes to get firm.

4 Using a sharp knife cut each pastry roll very thinly into 6 slices about the thickness of a pound coin, so that you have 48 slices in total. Place the slices on 2–3 baking trays.

5 Bake for 10–12 minutes until golden brown and crisp. Allow to cool in the trays for 5 minutes, then place the pastries on a wire rack to cool. These are best served warm.

6 If you prefer, you can cook these and chill in the fridge or freezer, then reheat for 5 minutes before serving.

 MARY'S WISE WORDS   *Don't use all-butter puff pastry as it can be a little soft to handle.*

CROQUE *Monsieur* TOASTS

MAKES 72 TINY
FINGER SHAPES

PREPARE AHEAD
The bread can be baked until
crisp up to 1 day in advance,
then topped with ham and
cheese an hour or two before
grilling rather than baking.

6 slices of thinly sliced
white bread (from a small,
ready-sliced loaf)

about 50g (2oz) melted butter

6 slices of smoked ham

150g (5oz) Gruyère cheese,
finely grated

2 tablespoons chopped parsley

You may need to make double quantities of these little bites
depending on how many guests you have, as in my experience
they're a very popular nibble and will have everyone coming back
for more and more.

1 Preheat the oven to 200°C/180°C fan/Gas 6.

2 Brush the slices of bread with the melted butter on both
sides. Place on a baking sheet and bake in the oven for about
15 minutes, turning over halfway through the cooking time.
The bread should be just crisp and lightly golden.

3 Remove the bread from the oven, but do not turn the oven off.
Put a slice of ham on top of each piece of bread and top evenly
with the grated cheese. Return the bread to the oven and bake
for about 10 minutes until the cheese has melted, then leave to
cool for 5 minutes.

4 Trim off the crusts and cut each slice of bread in half then slice
each half into 6 thin strips, so you get 12 fingers out of each slice.
Arrange the fingers on a large plate, sprinkle with parsley and
serve warm.

 MARY'S WISE WORDS   *Use Cheddar in this recipe if you prefer. If you wish, top each finger with a
strip of red pepper or tiny piece of sun-blushed tomato.*

GOAT'S CHEESE AND *Tomato* CANAPÉS

MAKES 24 CANAPÉS

PREPARE AHEAD

These can be prepared
2–3 hours in advance,
up to the point where
they're ready to go into
the oven, then baked
at the last minute.

12 dough balls

a little softened butter

1 x 150g pack soft goat's cheese

1 tablespoon red pesto

¼ teaspoon chopped
thyme leaves

12 cherry tomatoes, halved

25g (1oz) Parmesan cheese,
finely grated

salt and freshly ground
black pepper

A pack of ready-to-bake dough balls from your supermarket makes a very speedy base for these moreish nibbles.

1 Preheat the oven to 220°C/200°C fan/Gas 7. Line a baking sheet with baking paper.

2 Slice the dough balls in half and then cut a thin slice off the rounded side so both halves sit flat. Butter one side and arrange, buttered side down, on the baking sheet.

3 Mix the goat's cheese, pesto and thyme together in a small bowl. Spread this on to the unbuttered sides of the dough making sure that it is spread up to the edges, then place one tomato half on top.

4 Season then sprinkle over the Parmesan cheese. Bake for 10 minutes until crisp and lightly golden. Serve warm.

 MARY'S WISE WORDS   *If preferred, omit the tomatoes and use 100g (4oz) of sliced roasted red peppers from a jar instead.*

"Don't be shy about relying on certain ready-made products to help save you time"

ASIAN *Tuna* SKEWERS

MAKES ABOUT 30
SKEWERS

PREPARE AHEAD

You can marinate the
tuna for up to an hour
before cooking.

4 tablespoons soy sauce

2 tablespoons balsamic glaze

2 tablespoons sesame oil

2 tablespoons light
muscovado sugar

400g (14oz) piece of fresh tuna
or 2 x 200g (7oz) steaks

75g (3oz) sesame seeds, toasted

sunflower oil, for frying

This is a particularly good choice if you're serving a selection of
nibbles at your party. The flavours will contrast well with the likes
of little pastry bites, for example, and the elegant squares of
sesame-coated tuna look very smart and sophisticated yet are
so simple to prepare. Balsamic glaze is now available from good
supermarkets; it is a reduced balsamic vinegar blend and is great
for decorating plates too.

1 Measure the soy, balsamic glaze, sesame oil and sugar into
a bowl. Mix together then pour one half into a small bowl or
ramekin and set aside to use as a dipping sauce.

2 Cut the tuna into 4cm (1½in) cubes, then place in the marinade
in the bowl. Marinate for up to an hour if you have the time.

3 Pour sunflower oil into a large frying pan so it is 2cm (¾in)
deep. Heat over a high heat until a little piece of tuna sizzles
when added to the pan. Add the cubes of tuna and cook for
1–2 minutes only, until seared and just cooked. Do not overcook
or it will become dry. Remove from the pan with a slotted spoon.

4 Place the sesame seeds on a large plate then add the tuna and
toss to coat. Serve the tuna on cocktail sticks with the dip.

MARINATED *Prawns* WITH *Chilli Dip*

MAKES 24 PRAWNS

PREPARE AHEAD
You can marinate the
  prawns for up to an hour
  before cooking.

2 garlic cloves, crushed

½ mild red chilli,
  very finely chopped

grated zest and juice of 2 limes

2 tablespoons olive oil

24 raw, peeled king prawns
  (see Mary's Wise Words)

15g (½ oz) butter

FOR THE DIP

150ml (¼ pint) soured cream

2–3 tablespoons sweet
  chilli sauce

These mildly spiced prawns, handily served on little cocktail skewers, only need to be marinated very briefly then cooked at the last minute as they are best eaten hot. Provided all your cold canapés are ready, these can be the last ones you prepare, perhaps while any other hot ones are in the oven finishing cooking. Then you can leave your kitchen and spend time with your guests.

1 Place the garlic in a bowl with the chilli, lime zest and juice and 1 tablespoon of the oil. Add the prawns to the marinade 15 minutes before ready to cook, or for up to an hour if you have the time.

2 Meanwhile make the dip. Mix the soured cream and chilli sauce together and serve in a little bowl alongside the prawns.

3 Heat the remaining oil and the butter in a frying pan until hot and foaming. Fry half the prawns for 2–3 minutes over a high heat, turning once or twice until pink. Remove with a slotted spoon and set aside. Add the remaining prawns to the pan and cook in the same way. Return the other prawns to the pan and add any marinade that is still in the bowl. Heat for 30 seconds then serve the prawns on small bamboo skewers or cocktail sticks.

 MARY'S WISE WORDS

To de-vein prawns cut down the back and remove the black intestines with the point of a knife. Look for decorative bamboo skewers, which I buy in large supermarkets or over the internet. Also look out for frozen king prawns – allow to defrost for about 1 hour before marinating.

QUICK BITES AND CANAPÉS

SMOKED *Salmon* SKEWERS *with* DILL MUSTARD SAUCE

MAKES ABOUT
24 SKEWERS

PREPARE AHEAD
You can prepare both the salmon and the sauce up to 12 hours ahead. Cover tightly with clingfilm and keep refrigerated.

1 x 200g pack smoked salmon slices

1 tablespoon Dijon mustard

2 tablespoons white wine vinegar

4 tablespoons olive oil

1 tablespoon caster sugar

4 tablespoons light mayonnaise

1 tablespoon chopped dill

Canapés don't have to involve intricate and elaborate cooking. In fact the trick with them is their presentation: they simply have to look interesting and appealing. Smoked salmon is, with good reason, a staple of the canapé tray, yet coming up with original ways to serve it can flummox some cooks. Here's something new for you; it's easy to prepare in advance, too.

1 You will need 24 short bamboo sticks – about 15cm (6in) long. Cut the smoked salmon into strips – about three from each slice of salmon – then thread the strips on to the bamboo sticks so that they look pretty. Arrange on a serving platter.

2 Whisk the mustard, vinegar, oil and sugar together in a small bowl until combined, then whisk in the mayonnaise and dill. Season and spoon into a small serving bowl and place on the platter with the salmon.

SANDWICH *Skewers*

MAKES 9 SKEWERS

PREPARE AHEAD

Make these up to a day
ahead. Cover with a slightly
dampened sheet of kitchen
paper and wrap in clingfilm
until ready to serve.

a little softened butter

2 slices of thin-cut brown bread

4 slices of thin-cut white bread

1 slice of smoked salmon

1 teaspoon Dijon mustard

2 tablespoons mayonnaise

1 slice of ham

6 slices of peeled cucumber

Nothing could be simpler than making sandwiches, but when they are cut into tiny little squares and placed on a skewer they become such clever canapés and are ideal for all kinds of occasions, from drinks parties to children's parties. See photograph on previous page.

1 Lightly butter each slice of bread, then make a smoked salmon sandwich with the brown bread.

2 Mix the Dijon mustard with 1 tablespoon of the mayonnaise and spread over one slice of white bread. Top with the ham then another slice of white bread.

3 Spread the remaining tablespoon of mayonnaise on another slice of white bread. Top with the cucumber then the last piece of white bread.

4 Cut the crusts off all the sandwiches then cut each sandwich into 9 squares. Thread one ham, one salmon and one cucumber sandwich on to each skewer.

 MARY'S WISE WORDS

Don't be tempted to make sandwiches with messy fillings or anything too strongly flavoured as the combination needs to be very simple. You can buy clear plastic prism skewers for these canapés over the internet, or use skewers or long cocktail sticks.

TINY *Pesto* TARTLETS

**MAKES ABOUT
30 TARTLETS**

PREPARE AHEAD
These can be baked the day
before and just warmed
through at 220°C/200°C
fan/Gas 7 for 5 minutes
to re-crisp them.

1 x 320g pack ready-rolled
puff pastry

6 tablespoons basil or
sun-dried tomato pesto

2 roasted red peppers,
finely chopped

100g (4oz) feta
cheese, crumbled

basil leaves, to serve

Anything pastry-based, such as these little tartlets, is perfect
for parties. Not only does everyone love biting into crisp layers
of buttery, flaky pastry, but also these are small enough to help
soak up some of that pre-dinner tipple without filling your
guests ahead of the main event.

1 You will need 1–2 baking trays. Preheat the oven to
220°C/200°C fan/Gas 7.

2 Unroll the sheet of pastry and cut it vertically into strips 4cm
(1½in) wide, then cut horizontally to make 4cm (1½in) squares.
Place on the baking trays, with a little space in between them.

3 Place ¼ teaspoon of pesto in the centre of each tartlet. Top
with a little heap of chopped pepper and a piece of cheese; pile
as much filling into the centre of each square as possible, but
don't top the whole surface as the edges of each tart should rise
up around the filling.

4 Bake for 12–14 minutes until golden brown and risen.
Serve warm, topped with basil leaves.

 MARY'S WISE WORDS   *Try topping the tartlets with caramelised onions (see page 82) and
crumbled blue cheese and walnuts, or halved cherry tomatoes and tiny
pieces of diced chorizo.*

BLUE *Cheese* AND *Fig* FILO TARTLETS

MAKES 24 TARTLETS

PREPARE AHEAD
Bake the filo cases up to
  1 day ahead. Make the filling
  and chill in the fridge for up
  to 8 hours, then fill the cases
  on the day.

4 sheets of filo pastry
  measuring 25cm
  (10in) square
a little melted butter
3 ripe figs, chopped
  into small pieces
100g (4oz) creamy blue
  cheese, such as Dolcelatte
  or Roquefort
1 teaspoon lemon juice
3 sage leaves, chopped
ground mild paprika, to dust
freshly ground black pepper

These sophisticated little bites are deceptively simple to make – and most of the preparation can be done in advance.

1 Preheat the oven to 200°C/180°C fan/Gas 6. Grease a 24-hole mini muffin tray, or two 12-hole mini muffin trays, with melted butter.

2 Lay two filo sheets flat on a board and brush them with melted butter, then place one on top of the other. Cut into 25 equal squares about 5 x 5cm (2 x 2in). Repeat with the other two sheets. Put two squares on top of each other to make a star shape, and press into the prepared muffin tins. Repeat with the remaining sheets of pastry to make 24 mini tartlets (you will have one spare).

3 Divide the figs between the filo cases. Put the cheese, lemon juice and sage into a bowl. Mash down with a fork, season with pepper, then spoon blobs of cheese mixture on top of the figs. Sprinkle lightly with paprika and pepper.

4 Bake in the oven for 5–10 minutes until golden and crisp, and the cheese has just melted.

 MARY'S WISE WORDS

Ripe figs are delicious, but if they have tough skins, scoop the flesh away from the skin and chop. If figs are not in season use a pear, peeled and diced, then tossed in lemon juice.

Quail's Egg CROUSTADES WITH SPINACH AND *Hollandaise* SAUCE

MAKES 24
CROUSTADES

PREPARE AHEAD

Prepare and chop the spinach up to 1 day in advance. Cook the quail's eggs up to 1 day in advance, remove from the cold water and keep on a plate until needed.

100g (4oz) baby spinach leaves

24 quail's eggs

1 pack of mini croustade cases

about 6 tablespoons good hollandaise sauce

salt and freshly ground black pepper

a pinch of paprika, to serve

Having a packet of ready-made croustade cases in your store cupboard means that you've always got the basis of a quick and easy-to-make canapé on hand. You could substitute quail's eggs for smoked salmon or little pieces of crispy bacon, if preferred.

1 Place the spinach in a colander in the sink. Pour a kettle of boiling water over the spinach until wilted. Press out as much water as possible and pat dry with kitchen paper. Finely chop the spinach, adding a little salt and pepper. Set aside until required.

2 Bring a large pan of water to the boil. Have ready a bowl of cold water. Swirl the pan of boiling water with the handle end of a wooden spoon to create a sort of whirlpool, then break a quail's egg into a ramekin and slide it into the swirling water. Repeat this for 3–4 eggs at a time. Cook for about 1–2 minutes only – they should be just set but the yolks should still be runny. Remove from the pan with a slotted spoon then place in the bowl of cold water to stop them cooking any further. Repeat until all the eggs are cooked.

3 No more than 30 minutes before you want to serve the croustades, preheat the oven to 200°C/180°C fan/Gas 6. Once hot, divide the spinach between the croustade cases. Drain and pat the quail's eggs dry, trim off any loose egg white, then place one on top of each croustade case and pour over a little hollandaise sauce.

4 Cook in the oven for about 5 minutes or until just hot. Serve warm, sprinkled with paprika.

SHARING PLATES *and* STARTERS

Starters aren't something we necessarily enjoy on a daily basis but they're something I like to prepare for dinner parties or for special occasions. When deciding what sort of first course I want to serve, I tend to consider several factors. For me a starter should tempt the palate but not fill your guests up too much; it should always be a contrast to your main course rather than having ingredients that are too similar; and it should reflect the time of year and the produce that is in season.

Smoked salmon is always a popular choice as it's light and flavoursome and works throughout the year. In the spring I might serve Smoked Salmon with Potted Shrimps (page 68) while my Beetroot and Horseradish Gravadlax (page 79) is an ideal celebratory dish to serve for special occasions and parties, especially at Christmas. Gravadlax doesn't take long to prepare – you just have to allow a day or so for the curing – but looks stunning.

In winter I like to serve a warming soup such as my Creamy Celeriac Soup (page 89) or Thai-Spiced Tomato Soup (page 91) followed by a roast or casserole. These soups are also wonderful to serve for lunch with a warmed bread roll.

There is a fashion nowadays for putting a large platter of items in the centre of the table for everyone to tuck into. Of course it is easy to go and buy some cured meats, antipasti vegetables and dips, but I think it is nice to do some of the platter yourself, if time permits. If you prepare everything in advance it doesn't take long to assemble the platter (see page 92).

Your guests will very much appreciate the work that you have put into making their meal memorable, and I do hope you will enjoy making these dishes too.

SCALLOPS WITH *Lemon* AND DILL SAUCE AND *Watercress*

SERVES 6

2 large oranges

100g (4oz) watercress

6 large, fat scallops
    without the roe

65g (2½oz) butter

1 tablespoon olive oil

1 tablespoon lemon juice

1 tablespoon chopped dill

salt and freshly ground
    black pepper

You want to cook scallops so that they're still meltingly tender in the mouth – you should barely need to chew. It's very easy to overcook them, however, so you need to work quickly. Follow my tip below for how to avoid a rubbery texture. If you have hungry guests, or smaller scallops, allow two scallops per person.

1 Using a sharp knife cut the top and bottom off of each orange, then stand the oranges upright on a board and cut off all the peel and pith. Hold the oranges over a bowl to catch the drips and cut between each segment to release them. Arrange the orange segments on six serving plates with the watercress and set aside.

2 Slice each scallop into three discs and season well.

3 Heat 15g (½oz) of the butter and the olive oil in a frying pan over a high heat. When hot add the scallops and cook for just 1 minute, turn them over and cook for a further 30 seconds. You may need to cook them in batches. Remove with a slotted spoon and place on the plate with the watercress.

4 Add the remaining butter to the pan and allow to melt gently. Add the lemon juice and dill and a little seasoning then drizzle over the scallops and serve immediately.

 MARY'S WISE WORDS

To cook scallops, I add them one by one to the pan in a clockwise direction like the numbers on a clock, then when I need to turn them over, I start at the beginning and work around the pan so that the scallops are all cooked for the same length of time.

SMOKED SALMON *with* POTTED SHRIMPS

SERVES 6

6 thin slices of light rye bread

a little softened butter

300g (10oz) smoked
    salmon slices

100g (4oz) rocket leaves

3 x 50g pots of potted shrimps

pinch of grated nutmeg

2–3 teaspoons lemon juice

a little salad dressing

6 lemon wedges

One for the warmer weather – a lovely, light, salady starter that can be rustled up in next to no time, leaving you more time to spend with your guests or on preparing the main course.

1 Butter the bread and divide between six side plates, placing one slice in the centre of each plate.

2 Arrange two slices of smoked salmon on top of each slice of bread, making sure you get lots of height in the centre.

3 Arrange a little pile of rocket leaves on the side of each plate next to the salmon.

4 Scoop the potted shrimps into a small pan and warm until the butter has melted. Add a pinch of grated nutmeg and lemon juice to taste. Drizzle a little salad dressing over the rocket leaves. Spoon the potted shrimps over the salmon and serve with lemon wedges.

 MARY'S WISE WORDS

I like to use a fairly dense light-coloured rye bread, either cut from a loaf or bought pre-sliced in a packet. Don't use the dark pumpernickel as its strong flavour could overpower the salmon. I prefer to buy whole nutmeg kernels and grate a little whenever needed.

ASPARAGUS *Mousse*

SERVES 6

PREPARE AHEAD
Make and chill in the
  fridge for 2–3 days.

450g (1lb) asparagus spears
300ml (½ pint)
  whipping cream
½ garlic clove, crushed
50g (2oz) baby spinach leaves
1 egg, separated
1 tablespoon lemon juice
3 leaves of platinum grade
  leaf gelatine (see page 223)
salt and freshly ground
  black pepper
3 thin slices of lemon, halved

This delicately flavoured mousse is an impressive dinner party starter. It uses leaf gelatine, which I've written about in more detail on page 223.

The mousse is delicious served with green salad, melba toast, crackers or a little smoked salmon.

1 You will need six 150ml (¼ pint) ramekin dishes or moulds. Bring a shallow pan of water to the boil, add the asparagus and cook for 3 minutes only. Drain and immerse in cold water to stop it cooking further. Drain and pat dry. Cut about 4cm (1½in) off the tips of 12 spears and set the pretty tips aside for a garnish.

2 Place the cream in a small pan with the garlic and heat gently until hand hot. Add the spinach and allow to wilt. Place the cream mixture and the asparagus in a food processor and blend until almost smooth. Return the mixture to the pan and heat for 1 minute. Beat the egg yolk and add to the mixture along with the lemon juice. Mix to combine and season to taste.

3 Soak the gelatine in 150ml (¼ pint) cold water for 10 minutes. When softened, remove from the water, shake off excess water, add to the warm asparagus mixture and stir until dissolved. Pour the mixture into a shallow container and chill in the fridge for about 1½ hours until on the point of setting.

4 Whisk the egg white until it forms stiff peaks, then fold into the asparagus mixture. Divide the mixture between the six ramekins and leave to set in the fridge for at least 4 hours.

5 To turn out the mousses, dip the ramekins into boiling water for a second or two, then invert the moulds on to side plates and shake gently to release the mousse. Decorate each with 2 asparagus spears and a slice of lemon.

CRAB *Cocktail*

SERVES 6

PREPARE AHEAD

These can be prepared and kept in the fridge for about 2 hours before serving.

3 Little Gem lettuces, cored and finely shredded

8 plum tomatoes, halved, deseeded and cut into fine strips

3 spring onions, finely chopped

2 small avocados, diced

juice of 1 lime

3 tablespoons mayonnaise

2 tablespoons crème fraîche

a little finely chopped red chilli

1 teaspoon tomato ketchup

200g (7oz) fresh white crab meat

salt and freshly ground black pepper

a little coriander or flat-leaf parsley, to garnish

Swapping the customary prawns for crab lends this starter a little more elegance and sophistication, as to me the crab meat looks more delicate perched on top of the avocado. I know that there might be some prawn cocktail stalwarts among you who won't want to break from tradition, though, and you can easily substitute peeled prawns for crab (see Mary's Wise Words).

1 Divide the lettuce between six cocktail glasses or tumblers.

2 Set aside a few strips of tomato for garnish then mix the rest with the spring onions. Add the avocado, lime juice and a little seasoning. Stir well then pile on to the lettuce.

3 Mix the mayonnaise with the crème fraîche, chilli and ketchup. Season to taste then spoon over the avocado. Top with the crab meat and garnish with the remaining tomato strips and a coriander or parsley leaf.

 MARY'S WISE WORDS

Use 200g (7oz) peeled prawns instead of the crab, if preferred.

The dressing just needs a hint of chilli; if you don't have fresh chilli, use a little chopped chilli from a jar or a few dried chilli flakes.

GARLIC *Mussels* WITH A HINT OF *Lemon*

SERVES 6

2kg (4lb) fresh live mussels

a large knob of butter

1 large onion, chopped

¼ red chilli, deseeded
and diced

2 garlic cloves, crushed

150ml (¼ pint) dry white wine

150ml (¼ pint) pouring
double cream

2 tablespoons lemon juice

3 tablespoons chopped parsley

salt and freshly ground
black pepper

crusty bread, to serve

This is such a delicious, quick and easy recipe to make for a midweek supper or to share with friends. I like to add a little chilli for a touch of spiciness, but leave it out if you prefer. Simply serve with lots of crusty bread to mop up all the juices.

1 Tip the mussels into a large bowl of cold water. Check through them and throw away any that are open or do not close when tapped, as this means they are not fresh. Pull away the hairy beards, and scrape off any large barnacles but don't worry too much about cleaning them all off.

2 Melt the butter in a very large, deep saucepan or preserving pan. Add the onion and chilli, cover with a lid and cook over a low heat for about 5 minutes until just soft. Add the garlic and fry for 1 minute.

3 Add the mussels and toss over a high heat. Add the wine, cover with a lid and boil for about 5 minutes until all of the mussels have opened (discard any that haven't). Remove the lid and boil for a few minutes to reduce the liquid a little, then add the cream and lemon juice and season. Simmer for 3 minutes until slightly thickened. Add the parsley and serve piping hot in bowls with plenty of crusty bread.

 MARY'S WISE WORDS

It is a good idea to give each guest a little bowl of warm water with a slice of lemon in, to use as a rinsing bowl for their fingers. Place a couple of large empty bowls on the table for the shells, too.

MARY'S MENU FOR

A DINNER PARTY

APPETISERS

Blue Cheese and Fig Filo Tartlets

Goat's Cheese and Tomato Canapés

STARTER

Salmon and Asparagus Terrine

MAIN COURSE

Guinea Fowl with Wild Mushroom Sauce

Vegetable Platter

DESSERT

Warm Chocolate Fondant Tart

SALMON AND *Asparagus* TERRINE

SERVES 8

PREPARE AHEAD
This will keep for up to
  2 days in the fridge.

150g (5oz) salmon fillet

about 7 large asparagus spears

350g (12oz) smoked
  salmon slices

200g (7oz) full-fat
  cream cheese

75g (3oz) softened butter

1 tablespoon chopped chives

2 tablespoons lemon juice

salt and freshly ground
  black pepper

cress, to serve (optional)

A terrine is a striking and impressive dish to place on the table at the start of a meal. This one, made with salmon and asparagus, is surprisingly light and you also have the possibility of varying the thickness of the slices according to how much or how little food will follow it.

Serve the slices of terrine with melba toast, oatcakes or a little green salad.

1 Grease a 450g (1lb) loaf tin then line with a double layer of clingfilm. Preheat the oven to 180°C/160°C fan/Gas 4.

2 Place the salmon fillet on a square of foil. Season the salmon and fold the foil over the top to make a parcel. Cook in the oven for 12–15 minutes until the flesh has turned an opaque pink. Remove from the oven and leave to cool.

3 Trim the woody ends of the asparagus to exactly the length of the tin. Bring a frying pan of water to the boil and cook the asparagus spears for 3–4 minutes until they feel just tender when pierced with a knife, then drain and plunge into ice-cold water to cool. Drain and pat dry.

4 Trim a smoked salmon slice to fit the base of the tin then cut slices to fit all four sides, leaving a little to overhang, and reserve one slice for the top.

5 Place the remaining smoked salmon in a food processor with the cold cooked salmon fillet, cream cheese, soft butter, chives and lemon juice. Blend until smooth and season to taste.

Continues overleaf

6 Spread half the smoked salmon mixture into the lined tin and top with the asparagus spears, laying them head to tail so that they fit tightly into the tin. Top with the remaining salmon mixture and lay the last piece of smoked salmon on top.

7 Cover the terrine with clingfilm and leave to chill for at least 6 hours in the fridge, then remove the clingfilm, turn out and cut into slices (see Mary's Wise Words). Scatter with cress, if using, and serve.

 MARY'S WISE WORDS   *If you freeze the terrine for 30 minutes it will be easier to slice.*
You could also make this in individual 150ml (¼ pint) ramekins and turn them out, to create separate, portion-sized terrines for each person.

BEETROOT AND *Horseradish* GRAVADLAX

SERVES 8

PREPARE AHEAD

This can be made up
to 2 days in advance.

FREEZE

This freezes well, either as a
whole fillet or in portions or
slices. Make sure you wrap
it tightly in a double layer of
clingfilm and freeze for no
more than 1 month.

1kg (2 lb 2 oz) salmon fillet,
skin on

FOR THE CURE

2 tablespoons fresh
grated horseradish
(from a jar, if preferred)

200g (7oz) raw beetroot,
peeled and grated

75g (3oz) demerara sugar

75g (3oz) coarse sea salt

grated zest of 1 orange

freshly ground black pepper

**FOR THE
BEETROOT SALAD**

1 teaspoon Dijon mustard

1 tablespoon white
wine vinegar

3 tablespoons olive oil

1 teaspoon caster sugar

1 tablespoon chopped chives

500g (11b 2oz) cooked peeled
beetroot, finely diced

Curing salmon in beetroot and horseradish offers a twist on
the classic Scandinavian recipe. It makes for a beautiful first
course, not only because the beetroot stains the fish a stunning
dark purple; it also imbues the salmon with a delicate, subtle,
earthy flavour.

Gravadlax makes a lovely celebratory starter at any time of the
year, but I particularly like to serve it at Christmas. It's especially
handy then, as it's something you can prepare a couple of days
ahead or even freeze so that you have it on hand to serve as a
starter or with drinks when you need to.

Note that you will need to start preparing this dish at least
24–36 hours ahead.

1 Lay the salmon fillet skin-side down then remove any fine
bones with tweezers (run your fingers over the salmon to feel
them). This process is known as pinning, and the fishmonger
may already have done it for you.

2 Line a large roasting tin with foil. Put the salmon skin-side
down on to the foil.

3 Mix all of the curing ingredients together and spread over the
salmon flesh. Press down firmly to cover the surface. Cover the
tin with foil and seal the edges. Place another roasting tin on
top of the salmon then weigh it down with scale weights or cans
of pulses.

4 Put into the fridge for 24–36 hours. When ready, remove the
foil, scrape off the topping and carefully drain off all the sticky

Continues overleaf

FOR THE HORSERADISH SAUCE

3 tablespoons fresh grated horseradish (from a jar, if preferred)

200g (7oz) crème fraîche

TO SERVE

a few trimmed chive stems, to garnish

brown bread and butter

liquid. Wrap the salmon in a fresh piece of foil and store in the fridge until ready to serve.

5 To make the salad, measure the mustard, vinegar, oil and sugar into a bowl. Whisk together until smooth and season to taste. Add the chopped chives and beetroot and toss together.

6 To make the sauce, mix the horseradish and crème fraîche together in a bowl and season.

7 To serve, cut three thin slices of gravadlax per person, and arrange on eight individual plates. Serve with a pile of beetroot salad and a spoonful of sauce. Arrange the trimmed chive stems on top of the salmon and serve with brown bread and butter.

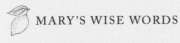 **MARY'S WISE WORDS**   *Buy the best salmon you can. If you can't buy fresh horseradish, look for jars of grated horseradish.*

TOMATO AND *Onion* GALETTES

MAKES 6 GALETTES

PREPARE AHEAD

These can be made and kept
in the fridge for 2–3 hours
before baking.

15g (½oz) butter

1 tablespoon olive oil

2 onions, finely sliced

2 tablespoons light
muscovado sugar

1 tablespoon balsamic vinegar,
plus extra, for drizzling

1 x 320g pack ready-rolled
puff pastry

200g (7 oz) cherry tomatoes,
each cut into 4 (you will
need 18 slices altogether)

a little grated Parmesan cheese

salt and freshly ground
black pepper

rocket leaves, to serve

A *galette* is a French creation – essentially a round, flat or free-form pastry, which is filled or topped with sweet or savoury ingredients. They are the cook and pastry-lover's great friend as the more rustic approach means they don't have to look as neat and tidy as one might expect a quiche to be, for example, and are very easy to throw together. I often serve these as a light lunch, perhaps after a bowl of soup or just with a green salad.

1 Heat the butter and oil in a pan and very gently fry the onions for about 5–8 minutes until transparent and tender. Add the sugar and balsamic vinegar and continue to cook until brown and sticky. Season with salt and black pepper to taste.

2 Preheat the oven to 220°C/200°C fan/Gas 7. Lightly grease a baking sheet. Lightly roll out the pastry and cut into 6 circles, about 15cm (6in) in diameter, using a saucer as a template. Transfer the circles to the baking sheet.

3 Divide the sticky onions between the circles. Arrange all the tomatoes on top of the tartlets. Sprinkle with the Parmesan and bake for 15 minutes until golden brown and risen. Serve with a few rocket leaves drizzled with balsamic vinegar.

 MARY'S WISE WORDS *Top the tartlets with slices of goat's cheese instead of the tomatoes, if preferred.*

"A starter should tempt the palate, but also reflect the time of year and the produce in season"

AVOCADO, TOMATO AND *Mint* SALAD

SERVES 6

PREPARE AHEAD
You can chop the tomatoes and toss them in the dressing up to 1 day in advance and chill in the fridge.

3 firm but ripe avocados, halved and stoned

6 ripe tomatoes, halved, deseeded and diced

FOR THE FRENCH DRESSING

1 tablespoon white wine or cider vinegar

2 tablespoons olive oil

½ teaspoon Dijon mustard

1 teaspoon mint sauce

1 teaspoon sugar

salt and freshly ground black pepper

mint leaves, to garnish

If you are looking for a starter to rustle up in minutes, this is your solution. I make this as my standby starter or sometimes as a light lunch for myself.

1 Start by making the dressing. Whisk the vinegar, oil, mustard and mint sauce together. Season with salt, pepper and a little sugar to taste.

2 Slice the avocado halves, then arrange each half in a fan shape on a side plate. Scatter the tomato over the avocado then drizzle over the dressing. Serve garnished with fresh mint leaves.

 MARY'S WISE WORDS *Give avocados a gentle squeeze in the palm of your hand – they should 'give' slightly but not be too hard or too soft. I often choose the ripe and ready-to-eat ones to be sure they have the best flavour. Remember that avocado will turn brown if exposed to the air, so coat with the dressing as quickly as possible.*

SHARING PLATES AND STARTERS

Thai-Spiced TOMATO SOUP

SERVES 6

PREPARE AHEAD

This can be made and kept in the fridge for up to 2 days.

FREEZE

Freeze for up to 1 month.

1 tablespoon olive oil

1 onion, chopped

2 carrots, chopped

1 red pepper, deseeded and chopped

1 tablespoon grated fresh ginger root

1 tablespoon red Thai curry paste

1 x 400g can chopped tomatoes

1 x 400g can coconut milk

1 lemongrass stick, bashed with a rolling pin

1 tablespoon tomato purée

1 tablespoon light muscovado sugar

2 tablespoons Thai basil leaves, chopped, plus extra leaves to decorate

This is an unusual spicy and fragrant soup, which is lovely to serve on a cold winter's day.

1 Heat the oil in a saucepan over a medium–high heat. Add the onion, carrots and red pepper and fry for 3 minutes. Add the ginger and Thai curry paste and fry for 30 seconds.

2 Add all the remaining ingredients except the Thai basil. Bring up to the boil, cover with a lid and simmer for 20 minutes until the vegetables are soft. Remove the lemongrass stalk, add the Thai basil then place the soup in a blender or food processor and purée until smooth.

3 Return the soup to the pan, add about 200ml (7fl oz) of water to thin the soup down, and reheat to serve. Decorate each bowl of soup with fresh Thai basil leaves.

 MARY'S WISE WORDS   *Thai basil, sometimes known as holy basil, is now available in supermarkets. Its large leaves are very fragrant with a distinctive citrusy and clove-like flavour that is delicious in Asian dishes.*

SERVES 8 AS PART OF A SHARING PLATTER

200g (7oz) blanched almonds

2 tablespoons olive oil

2 teaspoons sea salt

2 tablespoons finely chopped rosemary leaves

½ teaspoon smoked paprika

ROSEMARY ROASTED ALMONDS

1 Heat a wide-based pan over a very high heat and dry-fry the almonds for a minute until toasted. Watch them carefully as they can burn easily. Add the oil, salt and rosemary, reduce the heat and fry until crisp.

2 Remove from the heat and sprinkle in the paprika, toss together and serve.

3 Alternatively you can roast the almonds in an oven preheated to oven to 220°C/200°C fan/Gas 7. Place the almonds in a small ovenproof dish and drizzle with the oil. Sprinkle with the salt and paprika and roast in the oven for 15 minutes until golden brown. Sprinkle with the rosemary and serve warm or cold.

250g (9oz) white seed and
grain bread flour

1 teaspoon salt

1 teaspoon sugar

1 teaspoon easy-blend yeast

2 tablespoons olive oil

sesame or poppy seeds,
semolina or polenta, for
rolling the bread sticks

sea salt, to finish

SEEDED BREAD STICKS

If you don't have grain bread flour, use the same quantity of white bread flour and add two tablespoons of mixed seeds, such as sesame, sunflower and pumpkin seeds.

1 Lightly oil two baking trays. Measure the flour, salt and sugar into a mixing bowl and stir in the yeast. Mix the oil with 150ml (¼ pint) lukewarm water and add to the flour. Mix well until it forms a soft dough, then turn out on to the work surface and knead for 10 minutes (or for 4–5 minutes in a mixer with a dough hook).

2 Sprinkle the worktop with the sesame or poppy seeds, semolina or polenta and roll out the dough as thinly as possible into a rectangle – the seeds will stick to the outside of the dough. Cut the dough into 1cm (½in) wide strips. Then roll each one between your hands to a pencil shape, trying to make sure there are seeds all the way around each stick. Place on the baking tray, spaced a little apart. Cover with clingfilm and leave in a warm place to prove for about 15–20 minutes, until risen a little. Sprinkle with a little sea salt. Preheat the oven to 220°C/200°C fan/Gas 7.

3 Bake the bread sticks for 10 minutes until golden brown and crisp. They will be soft inside at this stage; if you prefer drier grissini-style sticks, bake for a further 3 minutes. Allow to cool completely, then store in a tin for up to 3 days.

2 x 400g cans
   chickpeas, drained

1 garlic clove, crushed

5 tablespoons extra
   virgin olive oil

grated zest and juice
   of 2 lemons

3 tablespoons Greek yoghurt

a good pinch of ground cumin

plenty of salt and ground
   black pepper

LEMON HOUMOUS

**If you like the traditional sesame seed flavour of houmous, add
three tablespoons of tahini paste to the mixture or, if you prefer,
add four tablespoons of chopped fresh coriander leaves for an
aromatic flavour.**

1 Place all the ingredients in a food processor with 2 tablespoons
of hot water and blend until smooth. Season to taste and pop in
the fridge to chill. Serve chilled.

250g (9oz) small ripe tomatoes
   on the vine, halved

250g (9oz) mini
   mozzarella balls

about 8 basil leaves,
   finely chopped

2 tablespoons olive oil

1 tablespoon balsamic vinegar

salt and freshly ground
   black pepper

CHERRY TOMATO AND MOZZARELLA SALAD

1 Place all the ingredients in a bowl, season well and chill until
ready to serve.

SERVES 8 AS PART
OF A SHARING
PLATTER, OR 4–6
AS A SIDE DISH

1 small aubergine, cut into
5mm (¼in) slices

1 courgette, cut into 5mm
(¼in) slices

3 red peppers, deseeded and
cut into 5mm (¼in) strips

2 red onions, thickly sliced

3 garlic cloves, crushed

2 tablespoons olive oil

200g (7oz) chargrilled
artichoke hearts in oil,
drained

2 teaspoons balsamic vinegar

salt and freshly ground
black pepper

ROASTED VEGETABLES

1 Preheat the oven to 220°C/200°C fan/Gas 7. Place all the
vegetables except the artichokes in a roasting tin with the garlic
and drizzle with oil. Season well.

2 Roast the vegetables for 20 minutes, then add the drained
artichoke hearts, toss everything together and return to the oven
for a further 5–10 minutes until hot and slightly charred. Allow
to cool.

3 When cool, toss the vegetables with balsamic vinegar and serve.

Family Favourites

FAMILY FAVOURITES

This chapter is made up of the recipes that I think of as 'family favourites'. By this, I mean not only that these meals are popular in my household, but also that they meet certain additional criteria.

A 'family favourite' could be a recipe that will feed and nourish hungry adults and children on a busy weeknight when I have less time to cook. So I have included recipes here that are quick to prepare, yet still tasty and filling, featuring store-cupboard staples such as pasta. Other family favourites are dishes such as risottos, quiches, curries and stews – meals that everybody is familiar with yet that never fail to delight.

Many of my recipes are versions of classic dishes that have been given a little twist – a simple cottage pie has been given a luxurious dauphinois topping (page 107) and burgers are made from pork and red pepper rather than the more traditional beef (page 118). And there are dishes that, while they are still meals I would serve up on a weeknight, are that little bit more special and for me they could also double up as casual supper party offerings.

RICH BEEF AND *Mushroom* STEW

PREPARE AHEAD
This can be cooked the day
before, chilled in the fridge
and reheated.

FREEZE
Cool completely then freeze
for up to 3 months. Defrost
in the fridge overnight and
reheat thoroughly.

50g (2oz) plain flour

2kg (4lb) shin of beef, cut
into 2.5cm (1in) chunks and
trimmed of any excess fat

6 tablespoons vegetable oil

6 small shallots,
peeled and kept whole

6 celery sticks, roughly sliced

8 carrots, roughly chopped

25g (1oz) dried
porcini mushrooms

600ml (1 pint) red
wine or stout

300ml (½ pint) beef stock

6 sprigs of thyme

450g (1lb) button mushrooms

2 tablespoons redcurrant jelly

salt and freshly ground
black pepper

This is a rich and comforting stew, smart enough to serve for a dinner party. I serve it with Mustard Mash (see page 105) and a green vegetable. Shin of beef has an excellent flavour but needs slow cooking – for an alternative, look for braising steak.

1 Place the flour in a bowl or in a plastic bag with plenty of salt and black pepper and toss the meat in it until well coated.

2 Heat the oil in a large flameproof casserole and add the beef. Fry until browned on all sides. You may need to do this in batches as you don't want to overcrowd the pan; it is important to just brown the beef and not stew it. Remove the meat from the pan using a slotted spoon and set aside. Add the shallots, celery and carrots to the pan and fry for 5 minutes until softened a little.

3 Meanwhile, soak the dried mushrooms in 300ml (½ pint) boiling water until softened, then chop into smaller pieces, reserving the soaking liquid.

4 Return the meat to the pan and add the red wine or stout. Bring to the boil and bubble for 4–5 minutes, until reduced by about a third, then add the stock, the soaked mushrooms and their soaking liquid and the thyme. Bring back to the boil then cover and simmer on a low heat for about 2½ hours or until tender. If preferred, you can place the dish in a preheated oven at 150°C/130°C fan/Gas 3 to cook for the same amount of time.

5 Add the button mushrooms to the casserole with the redcurrant jelly and continue to cook for a further 30 minutes or until the meat is meltingly tender.

 MARY'S WISE WORDS

If you want to thicken the sauce further, mix 1 tablespoon of plain flour with 2–3 tablespoons of cold water to make a thin paste, and add gradually to the boiling sauce until thickened to your liking. To help get the skins off the shallots, soak in boiling water before peeling.

Mustard MASH

SERVES 4–6

1.5kg (3lb) floury potatoes,
    peeled and cut into chunks

50g (2oz) butter

100ml (4fl oz) milk

2 tablespoons
    wholegrain mustard

A dash of wholegrain mustard never fails to liven up a dish of good old mashed potato. I like to serve this with my Rich Beef and Mushroom Stew (see page 102), but you could equally serve this alongside a Sunday roast.

1 Put the potatoes into a pan of cold salted water. Bring up to the boil and boil gently for about 20 minutes, or until the potatoes feel really tender.

2 Drain the potato chunks well, then return to the pan. Add the butter and milk, and mash using a potato masher until no lumps remain. Season with salt and pepper, if needed. Add the wholegrain mustard to the potato, and stir to combine.

3 To serve, spoon into a warmed serving dish and serve immediately.

 MARY'S WISE WORDS

Cutting the potatoes into evenly shaped chunks means that they will cook in the same amount of time. This makes it much easier to know when they are ready to take off the heat.

COTTAGE PIE WITH
Dauphinois POTATO TOPPING

SERVES 6–8

PREPARE AHEAD
The minced beef mixture can be cooked 1–2 days in advance.

FREEZE
The cooked mince mixture can be frozen for up to 3 months.

1 tablespoon sunflower oil

900g (2lb) minced beef

2 onions, chopped

4 celery sticks, diced

50g (2oz) plain flour

250ml (9fl oz) red wine

300ml (½ pint) beef stock

2 tablespoons Worcestershire sauce

2 tablespoons light muscovado sugar

1 tablespoon chopped thyme

250g (9oz) small chestnut mushrooms, sliced

dash of gravy browning (optional)

1.5kg (3lb) King Edward potatoes, peeled and cut into 4mm slices

150ml (¼ pint) pouring double cream

100g (4oz) strong Cheddar cheese, grated

salt and freshly ground black pepper

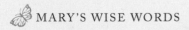 MARY'S WISE WORDS

A luxurious layer of cream and potato make this 'dauphinois' version so much smarter than the usual cottage pie, yet it's just as easy to prepare. And it tastes great the next day too.

1 You will need a 2-litre (3½-pint) shallow ovenproof dish. Heat the oil in a large frying pan until hot. Fry the beef over a high heat until golden brown, stirring, then remove from the pan and set aside. Add the onion and celery to the pan and fry until beginning to soften. Return the beef to the pan.

2 Whisk the flour and wine together in a bowl to make a smooth paste. Whisk in the stock then add to the pan with the Worcestershire sauce, sugar and thyme. Bring to the boil, stirring until thickened, then add the mushrooms and gravy browning, if using, and season. Cover with a lid and simmer for 45 minutes, until the mince is tender, then check the seasoning.

3 Preheat the oven to 220°C/200°C fan/Gas 7. Cook the potato slices in boiling salted water for about 4–5 minutes – they need to be just soft. Drain carefully in a colander and leave to cool a little. Don't worry if the potatoes break up a little, as this will help them absorb the cream; if they are too hard they will be waxy and the cream will run off.

4 Tip the cooked meat into the ovenproof dish. Arrange a layer of the blanched potato on top of the mince, then pour over half the cream. Arrange the remaining potato on top, seasoning between the layers, then pour over the remaining cream and sprinkle over the cheese. Bake in the oven for about 30 minutes or until golden and bubbling.

Make sure you cook the dish fairly quickly once the potato topping is added or the potatoes may discolour and the cream will sink into the meat.

RIB-EYE STEAK WITH *Stilton* BUTTER

SERVES 6

100g (4oz) softened butter

2 banana shallots, finely diced

75g (3oz) Stilton

1 tablespoon finely
    chopped chives

a little olive oil

6 x 4cm- (1½in-) thick
    rib-eye steaks, each
    about 200g (7oz)

salt and freshly ground
    black pepper

A thick, juicy steak is a real treat and so easy to cook for a dinner party, and here's how to cook them without having to disappear to the kitchen at the last minute or fill the room with smoke!

1 Melt 25g (1oz) of the butter in a small pan and cook the shallots over a low heat until softened. Remove from the heat, tip into a bowl and allow to cool for 10 minutes.

2 Mash the Stilton with a fork and beat in the remaining butter and the chives. Add the shallot mixture and season with salt and pepper. Mix well.

3 Place the Stilton butter on a sheet of clingfilm and form into a sausage shape. Roll up, twisting the ends to secure. Chill for at least 30 minutes before using.

4 Preheat the oven to 220°C/200°C fan/Gas 7. To cook the steaks, heat a large non-stick frying pan over a high heat. Brush each steak with a little oil and season with salt and pepper. Fry each steak for 2 minutes on each side or until golden and sealed. You will need to cook the steaks two or three at a time. Transfer to a baking sheet while you cook the remainder.

5 Bake the steaks for 6 minutes or until piping hot for rare. Add an extra 2 minutes for medium, and 4 minutes for medium to well done. Rest the steaks for 2 minutes. Slice the butter and place a slice on top of each steak just before serving.

 MARY'S WISE WORDS

If you are using fillet steak, this is totally lean, so use slightly less per person – around 150g (5oz) should be sufficient.

To cook the steak to perfection, make sure it sizzles as soon as it hits the hot pan and time the cooking for just 2 minutes on each side. The method above works well for any type of steak of the same thickness, but if using a thicker fillet steak, bake for 8 minutes for rare. Add 2 minutes for medium, and 4 minutes for medium to well done. Rest the steaks for 2 minutes before serving.

LAMB *Dhansak*

SERVES 6

PREPARE AHEAD
Make 1–2 days ahead, keep
in the fridge, then reheat
thoroughly.

FREEZE
Transfer to a freezer-proof
container and freeze for
1 month. Don't freeze for
longer as the flavours will
intensify and the dish may
become too spicy.

3 tablespoons sunflower oil

1kg (2lb 2oz) diced lamb
(shoulder or leg, or a mixture)

2 onions, diced

25g (1oz) fresh ginger
root, peeled but left whole

4 garlic cloves, peeled but
left whole

1 red chilli, deseeded
and chopped

10 green cardamom pods

1½ tablespoons ground cumin

1½ tablespoons
ground coriander

½ tablespoon ground turmeric

1 x 400g can chopped tomatoes

200ml (7fl oz) beef stock

75g (3oz) dried red lentils

3 tablespoons clear honey

salt and freshly ground
black pepper

Dhansak is a popular Indian curry made from meat and lentils,
flavoured with spices including cumin and ginger. It is mild,
sweet and rich with just enough heat to satisfy most tastes.
And best of all it benefits from being made a day in advance as
it tastes even better the next day. I like to serve this with Raita
and Fresh Tomato Relish (see page 112), as well as hard-boiled
eggs, poppadoms, rice and, of course, mango chutney.

1 Preheat the oven to 150°C/130°C fan/Gas 2.

2 Heat 2 tablespoons of the oil in a large frying pan. Add half the
lamb and fry until browned. Remove from the pan with a slotted
spoon and set aside, then brown the other half of the lamb and
set aside.

3 Add the remaining oil to the pan. Add the onions and fry for
4–5 minutes until beginning to soften.

4 Meanwhile, place the ginger, garlic and chilli into a small food
processor and whizz until finely chopped.

5 Bash the cardamom pods with the end of a rolling pin to
split the husks, then remove the seeds and grind them to a fine
powder in a pestle and mortar. Add to the pan along with the
remaining spices and the garlic and ginger mixture.

6 Add the remaining ingredients to the pan and add the lamb.
Bring to the boil, then cover and place in the oven to simmer for
1–2 hours until tender. Check the seasoning and serve.

Continues overleaf

A KITCHEN SUPPER

STARTER

Sharing Platter

MAIN COURSE

Lamb Dhansak

or

*Butternut Squash and
Spinach Lasagne*

DESSERT

Elderflower Posset

15-MINUTE *Pasta*

350g (12oz) penne pasta

2 tablespoons vegetable oil

2 x 80g packs Parma ham, snipped into small pieces

250g (9oz) small chestnut mushrooms, halved or quartered

200g (7oz) full-fat crème fraîche

100g (4oz) Parmesan cheese, grated

2 tablespoons chopped parsley

salt and freshly ground black pepper

green salad and crusty bread, to serve (optional)

This is my standby pasta supper – great for everyday family meals or for casual supper parties too. If you don't have Parma ham, then Black Forest ham or Serrano ham work just as well.

1 Cook the pasta in boiling salted water according to the packet instructions, drain and set aside.

2 Heat the oil in a frying pan. Add half the Parma ham and fry until crisp, then remove and set aside.

3 Add the mushrooms to the pan and fry for 2 minutes. Add the crème fraîche and bring up to the boil. Add the pasta, Parmesan, remaining ham and parsley and toss together over the heat. Season well. Serve topped with the crispy Parma ham, and with a green salad and crusty bread, if you like.

 MARY'S WISE WORDS

If you have left over double cream, you can use this instead of crème fraîche. For special occasions add a pack of asparagus tips to the pasta 4 minutes before the end of cooking time, then drain with the pasta.

　　FAMILY FAVOURITES

PORK AND *Red Pepper* BURGERS

MAKES 8 BURGERS

PREPARE AHEAD
The burgers can be prepared
and kept in the fridge for
2 days before cooking.

FREEZE
The burgers can be made
and frozen uncooked for
1 month. Layer them
between sheets of baking
paper in a freezer-proof
container so they will
separate easily. Defrost
thoroughly before cooking.

1 tablespoon sunflower oil

½ onion, finely diced

3 rashers of smoked streaky
bacon, finely chopped

1 garlic clove, crushed

75g (3oz) crustless bread

2 tablespoons finely
chopped parsley

450g (1lb) minced pork

2 roasted red peppers
(from a jar), drained

½ teaspoon salt

freshly ground black pepper

Serving a good homemade burger at a barbecue or for a kitchen supper makes such a change from bringing out ready-made versions. I think these pork burgers are a lovely alternative to a traditional beef burger, with lots of interesting flavours. Serve them with a crusty roll or some sweet potato chips.

1 Heat the oil in a frying pan and fry the onion and bacon over a low heat until the onion has completely softened but not browned. Add the garlic and fry for 1 minute.

2 Place the bread and parsley in a food processor, whizz to make crumbs, then add the onion and bacon mixture, pork, red peppers, salt and plenty of black pepper. Whizz until well mixed. Shape the mixture into 8 burgers and chill for 30 minutes if you have the time.

3 Preheat a grill or barbecue and when hot, grill the burgers for about 6–8 minutes on each side until golden and cooked through. Or cook in a little hot oil in a frying pan, and once browned reduce the heat and cook right through.

 MARY'S WISE WORDS

It is important to cook burgers right the way through, so I often brown them first then finish them off in a hot oven (200°C/180°C fan/Gas 6) for a further 5 minutes so that they cook without burning on the outside.

"A good homemade burger at a barbecue or for a kitchen supper makes such a change from ready-made versions"

PEPPERED *Tarragon* CHICKEN

SERVES 6

PREPARE AHEAD
The dish can be prepared
and kept in the fridge for
24 hours before roasting.

6 skinless, boneless
chicken breasts

1 x 150g pack black-pepper
full-fat cream cheese
(see Mary's Wise Words)

1 egg yolk

3 tablespoons chopped
tarragon, plus extra leaves,
to decorate

12 slices of Parma ham

a knob of butter

a little clear honey

200g (7 oz) full-fat
crème fraîche

juice of ½ lemon

salt and freshly ground
black pepper

I've had people tell me they are reluctant to cook chicken breasts because they worry they're going to be dry. But wrapping the chicken breasts in Parma ham will keep their juices locked into the meat. Couple that with a deliciously creamy stuffing and there's no chance of any dryness.

1 Preheat the oven to 200°C/180°C fan/Gas 6.

2 Put the chicken breasts on to a board. Using a sharp knife make a pocket in the side of the chicken breast, cutting through to the middle.

3 Mix the cream cheese with the egg yolk and 2 tablespoons of the tarragon and season well. Divide between the chicken breast pockets, pushing the mixture into each one. Wrap each breast in two slices of Parma ham so the chicken is completely covered.

4 Grease a small roasting tin with butter then arrange the chicken breasts inside. Drizzle over a little honey then roast for about 30–35 minutes or until the chicken is golden brown and no longer pink in the centre. Remove the chicken breasts from the tin and leave to rest for 5 minutes while you make the sauce.

5 Add the crème fraiche and lemon to the roasting tin. Put the tin on to the hob and bring to the boil, scraping the tin with a wooden spoon to release all of the chicken juices. Add the remaining chopped tarragon and season. Serve the chicken sprinkled with a few tarragon leaves, and with the sauce alongside for everyone to help themselves.

 MARY'S WISE WORDS

Look for firm, flavoured cream cheese rather than the very smooth type sold in plastic tubs. Smooth cream cheese may soften too much and run out of the chicken pockets before the meat is cooked.

To check that the chicken is cooked through, cut one breast in half – serve this one to yourself.

SPINACH, *Gruyère* AND HAM QUICHE

SERVES 8

PREPARE AHEAD
This will keep for up to 3 days
in the fridge once cooked.

FREEZE
Wrap the cooked quiche
in clingfilm and foil and
freeze for up to 1 month.
Defrost overnight.

FOR THE PASTRY
175g (6oz) plain flour, plus
  extra for dusting
100g (4oz) butter, cubed
1 egg, beaten
1 tablespoon water

FOR THE FILLING
a knob of butter
1 onion, chopped
200g (7oz) baby spinach
4 eggs, beaten
300ml (½ pint) double cream
100g (4oz) ham, diced
100g (4oz) Gruyère or
  Emmental cheese, grated
salt and freshly ground
  black pepper

Sometimes the simplest additions or tweaks to a basic recipe can really change the flavour of a dish. Here, using a strong-flavoured tangy cheese, such as Gruyère, really lifts this quiche and, in my opinion, makes it one of the tastiest ever.

1 You will need a deep, 23cm (9in) loose-bottomed fluted flan tin, a baking tray and baking beans. Preheat the oven to 200°C/180°C fan/Gas 6.

2 To make the pastry, measure the flour and butter into a food processor. Whizz until the mixture resembles breadcrumbs (or place in a mixing bowl and rub the butter into the flour with your fingertips). Add the egg and water to the dry mixture and mix until it forms a soft but not sticky dough.

3 Dust a work surface lightly with flour and roll out the pastry to a circle large enough to line the base and sides of the tin. Press on to the base and sides and trim the top edge. Prick the base all over with a fork. Line the pastry case with baking paper and baking beans. Bake in the oven for 10 minutes until just coloured, remove the beans and foil and bake for a further 5 minutes to dry out.

4 Reduce the oven temperature to 180°C/160°C fan/Gas 4. Place a heavy baking sheet in the oven to preheat.

5 To make the filling, melt the butter in a frying pan and gently fry the onion for about 5 minutes or until softened.

Continues overleaf

6 Place the spinach in a colander in the sink, then pour a kettle of boiling water over the spinach until it wilts. Squeeze out as much water as possible and pat the spinach with kitchen towel.

7 Beat the eggs and cream together and season with salt and black pepper.

8 Place the onion in the pastry case then top with the ham and spinach. Pour over the cream and egg mixture and sprinkle with the cheese.

9 Place the tin on the preheated baking tray and bake in the oven for 25–30 minutes until golden brown and just set in the centre.

 MARY'S WISE WORDS

For vegetarians simply omit the ham and make sure you use a strong-flavoured melting vegetarian cheese. Check the label – many cheeses are now made without animal rennet but there are many that still use it.

HOBIE'S *Tuna* PASTA BAKE

SERVES 6

PREPARE AHEAD

This can be prepared up to a day ahead then baked in the oven for about 20 minutes or until thoroughly hot all the way through.

FREEZE

This can be frozen for up to 1 month, but leave out the hard-boiled eggs as they will become rubbery when frozen. Don't sprinkle over the cheese topping – add the cheese after defrosting, just before you bake the dish.

250g (9oz) pasta shapes

50g (2oz) butter

50g (2oz) plain flour

600ml (1 pint) milk

100g (4oz) Cheddar cheese, grated

6 eggs

1 x 185g can tuna in oil, drained

1 x 195g can sweetcorn, drained

salt and freshly ground black pepper

Hobie, aged 6, and Louis, aged 8, are our grandsons. They love to cook this with me for our supper. Not only is it very simple to make but is also very tasty – both adults and children love it – and a great last-minute meal as you will probably have all the ingredients in your fridge or store cupboard already.

1 Preheat the oven to 200°C/180°C fan/Gas 6.

2 Bring a large pan of salted water to the boil, add the pasta and cook for 10–11 minutes or according to the packet instructions, until tender. Drain well.

3 Meanwhile, melt the butter in a small pan, whisk in the flour and cook for 1 minute. Gradually whisk in the milk, stirring until smooth and thickened. Season with salt and black pepper and add most of the cheese.

4 Cook the eggs in boiling water for 8 minutes, then plunge them into cold water to cool. Remove the egg shells and cut the eggs into quarters.

5 Mix the pasta with the cheese sauce, then add the eggs, flaked tuna and sweetcorn and turn into a baking dish. Sprinkle with the remaining cheese and bake for 20 minutes until browned. Alternatively, if serving at once, the hot dish can be browned under the grill instead of being placed in the oven.

 MARY'S WISE WORDS

If you wish, you can use frozen sweetcorn instead of tinned, or replace them with peas, if preferred.

BUTTERNUT SQUASH
AND *Spinach* LASAGNE

SERVES 6

1 small butternut squash,
  peeled, seeds removed and
  cut into 3–4cm chunks

2 onions, thickly sliced

2 tablespoons olive oil

250g (9oz) button chestnut
  mushrooms, sliced thickly

250g (9oz) spinach, washed

about 6 large dried
  lasagne sheets

salt and freshly ground
  black pepper

FOR THE
TOMATO SAUCE

400ml (¾ pint) tomato passata

3 tablespoons red pesto

FOR THE
CHEESE SAUCE

75g (3oz) butter

75g (3oz) plain flour

600ml (1 pint) hot milk

2 teaspoons Dijon mustard

200g (7oz) Gruyère
  cheese, grated

This is a great combination of colourful vegetables that makes a rich and satisfying vegetable supper. For vegetarians use a well-flavoured vegetarian cheese. Lasagne sheets vary in size, so aim to have two layers of pasta to fit the dish without overlapping.

1 Preheat the oven to 200°C/180°C fan/Gas 6. You will need a shallow 2-litre (3½-pint) shallow baking dish.

2 Place the squash and onions in a roasting tin, mix with the oil, season then roast for about 30 minutes until tender. (When you pierce the squash with a knife it should go through easily, but you don't want the squash to be mushy.) Add the mushrooms for the last 10 minutes.

3 Put the spinach in a colander in the sink, and pour over a kettle of boiling water until the spinach has wilted. Allow to drain, then press out as much of the water as you can.

4 For the tomato sauce, mix the tomato passata with the pesto.

5 Immerse the lasagne sheets in boiling water for 5 minutes until softened.

6 For the cheese sauce, melt the butter in a small pan then beat in the flour. Gradually whisk in the hot milk, stirring all the time, until the sauce thickens. Add the mustard and about three quarters of the cheese and continue to stir gently until the cheese has melted. Season well.

Continues overleaf

You can make the components
of this – the vegetables and
sauces – one day ahead, or
make the whole dish one day
ahead and chill in the fridge
either uncooked or cooked.
If cooked, reheat the dish
covered in foil so that the
top doesn't burn.

FREEZE

This is best frozen when
cooked. Defrost in the
fridge overnight before
reheating for 30–40 minutes
at 200°C/180°C fan/Gas 6.
Add at least 15–20 minutes
to this time if reheating
from frozen.

7 To assemble the lasagne, put a third of the roasted vegetables
into the bottom of your ovenproof dish followed by a layer of
spinach then a third of the tomato sauce and a third of the cheese
sauce. Lay lasagne sheets on top of this. Top with half of the
remaining vegetables, tomato sauce and cheese sauce. Add the
last lasagne sheets and top with the remaining vegetables, tomato
sauce and cheese sauce. Sprinkle the reserved cheese over the top.

8 Bake for 30–40 minutes or until the lasagne is golden and
bubbling on top.

 MARY'S WISE WORDS   *Many cheeses are now made with non-animal rennet, so always check the label
to check that it is suitable for vegetarians.*

PASTITSIO

SERVES 6

PREPARE AHEAD
This can be made 1–2 days in advance and chilled in the fridge. Bake in the oven for 30–40 minutes until piping hot in the centre.

FREEZE
Prepare up to step 5, and then freeze for up to 1 month. Defrost thoroughly then cook for 45 minutes in the oven at 220°C/200°C fan/Gas 7.

200g (7oz) macaroni

500g (1lb 2oz) lean minced lamb

1 tablespoon olive oil

2 onions, finely chopped

2 garlic cloves, crushed

25g (1oz) plain flour

150ml (¼ pint) red wine

1 x 400g can chopped tomatoes

1 tablespoon chopped marjoram

1 tablespoon tomato purée

1 tablespoon light muscovado sugar

2 bay leaves

salt and freshly ground black pepper

FOR THE SAUCE
25g (1oz) butter

25g (1oz) plain flour

300ml (½ pint) hot milk

2 teaspoons Dijon mustard

150g (5oz) mature Cheddar cheese, grated

This is a traditional Greek pasta bake using minced lamb, and is a great family supper dish. You could use penne pasta if you haven't any macaroni to hand.

1 Preheat the oven to 220°C/200°C fan/Gas 7. You will need a deep 2–2.25 litre (3½–4 pint) ovenproof dish.

2 Cook the macaroni in boiling salted water according to the packet instructions until al dente. Drain and refresh in cold water.

3 Heat a large non-stick frying pan or flameproof casserole. Dry-fry the lamb until browned then transfer to a plate. Heat the oil in the pan. Add the onions and garlic and fry for 5 minutes until soft, then return the lamb to the pan and sprinkle over the flour. Stir to coat the lamb in the flour. Blend in the remaining ingredients and season well. Cover with a lid, bring up to the boil and gently simmer on the hob for 30 minutes, until the lamb is tender. Remove the bay leaves.

4 While the mince is cooking, make the cheese sauce. Melt the butter in a saucepan and add the flour. Using a whisk, blend in the hot milk, whisking until smooth and thickened. Add the mustard and simmer for 30 seconds. Remove from the heat and add half the cheese. Season well.

5 Spoon half of the mince mixture into the ovenproof dish. Put half of the pasta on top and spread to cover the surface. Top with the remaining mince and pasta and then finish with the cheese sauce. Sprinkle the remaining cheese on top.

6 Bake in the oven for 25–30 minutes until bubbling and golden brown on top.

CHARGRILLED *Citrus* CHICKEN BREASTS

SERVES 4

PREPARE AHEAD
Marinate for no more than
1 day in the fridge. Or cook
completely and serve cold.

4 skinless, boneless chicken
breasts, cut into thick strips

grated zest and juice
of 1 lime

grated zest and juice
of 1 small orange

grated zest and juice
of 1 lemon

2 tablespoons clear honey

2 tablespoons olive oil

salt and freshly ground
black pepper

A quick and tasty way to serve chicken for a light summer lunch alongside plenty of salad. Try serving it with the Fiery Red Rice and Carrot Salad on page 208.

1 Place the chicken strips in a non-metallic bowl and pour over the citrus zest and juices and honey, and season. Leave in the fridge to marinate for about 1 hour.

2 Heat the oil in a non-stick frying pan. Lift the chicken out of the marinade, shaking off most of the grated zest and juice but reserving them, then fry the chicken for about 2–3 minutes, in batches if necessary, turning over halfway through, until browned and cooked through. Remove the chicken with a slotted spoon and transfer to a plate.

3 Add the reserved marinade to the pan and bring to the boil. Return the chicken to the pan, coat with the marinade and cook for just 1 minute until piping hot. Serve immediately.

SPICED *Garden* VEGETABLE CASSEROLE

SERVES 10

PREPARE AHEAD
You can cook this up to
2 days in advance. Not
suitable for freezing.

6 tablespoons vegetable oil

4 onions, roughly chopped

4 garlic cloves, crushed

2 teaspoons ground turmeric

2 x 400g cans plum tomatoes

2 large butternut squash,
peeled, deseeded and cut
into 2cm chunks

2 cauliflowers, broken into
small florets

4 red peppers, deseeded and
cut into 1cm pieces

2 x 400g cans
chickpeas, drained

600ml (1 pint)
vegetable stock

2 tablespoons harissa paste

2 tablespoons coriander
leaves, roughly chopped

salt and freshly ground
black pepper

**This casserole packs a punch in terms of flavour, and with
every forkful you can feel it doing you good! It is packed with
vegetables and pulses and is also low in fat but feels very filling.
It may sound strange but it is delicious served cold too.**

1 Preheat the oven to 160°C/140°C fan/Gas 3.

2 Heat the oil in a large flameproof casserole, and fry the onions
for about 5–8 minutes over a low heat until soft and transparent.
Add the garlic and turmeric and fry for 30 seconds.

3 Add the tomatoes, squash, cauliflower and peppers. Stir well
then add the chickpeas and stock. Bring to the boil, then cover
with a lid and cook in the oven for 1 hour, until all the vegetables
are really tender.

4 Remove a couple of tablespoonfuls of the juices, blend with the
harissa and stir back through the casserole. Taste and adjust the
seasoning. Add the coriander and serve hot.

 MARY'S WISE WORDS

*Harissa is a hot pepper and spice paste used in North African dishes. Recipes
vary, but it usually contains chillies, garlic, cumin, coriander and lemon. It can
vary in strength, so use with caution. It gives a rich intensity to all kinds of
casseroles and stews, is delicious stirred into houmous and can be rubbed on to
chicken before roasting too.*

Spectacular Suppers

SPECTACULAR SUPPERS

Of course, each person's notion of what makes a 'spectacular' supper
will be different. Perhaps it's the atmosphere during the evening, a
superb bottle of wine, a luxurious ingredient in the dish, or simply
a plate of food shared with loved ones – for me, these would all
make a supper truly spectacular.

This chapter is centred on food that I serve when I entertain. In
choosing the recipes, I thought about dishes that are special because
they make a memorable meal for my guests – this is either because
they're something a little unusual, or because in putting them on
the table I know they leave an impression, both visually and, most
importantly, with their flavour. There are recipes that might feature
ingredients that are a little bit more costly than I would normally
use – whole sea bass is not something I buy every day, but for a special
occasion I think it's lovely to splash out – and recipes that take more
time to prepare, such as an absolutely stunning Salmon en Croûte with
Pesto-Roasted Vegetables (page 150).

Entertaining doesn't need to be complicated, however. As in all the
chapters in this book, I've included as many dishes that can be partly
or fully prepared in advance, leaving you to enjoy the maximum
amount of time with your guests.

VENISON AND *Chestnut* PIE

SERVES 6

PREPARE AHEAD

The venison filling can be cooked, cooled and chilled for up to 2 days in the fridge before completing the pie.

FREEZE

Make the filling and allow to cool completely before transferring to a large lidded freezer-proof container and freezing for up to 1 month. Defrost completely before adding the pastry topping and cooking as from step 5.

5 tablespoons sunflower oil

2 onions, roughly chopped

6 rashers of streaky bacon, snipped into strips

750g (1¾lb) stewing venison, cut into cubes

50g (2oz) plain flour

4 tablespoons Madeira or medium sherry

450ml (¾ pint) red wine

450ml (¾ pint) beef stock

2 tablespoons wholegrain mustard

300g (11oz) chestnut mushrooms, quartered

1 x 200g (7oz) pack whole peeled, cooked chestnuts

3 bay leaves

4 sprigs of thyme

500g (1lb 2oz) puff pastry

1 egg, beaten

salt and freshly ground black pepper

This is a hearty dish to serve on a cold autumn evening or for Sunday lunch with loads of buttery mashed potato and green vegetables. The filling is simply a rich venison stew so you could also serve it without the pastry if you prefer.

1 You will need a deep 2.25-litre (4-pint) pie dish. Heat 2 tablespoons of the oil in a large shallow pan or frying pan that has a lid and cook the onions for 5 minutes, until soft and transparent. Add the bacon and cook for a further 5 minutes.

2 Remove the onions and bacon from the pan using a slotted spoon and set aside. Add the remaining oil and when hot add the venison and fry until browned. You will need to do this in batches so that the meat browns rather than stews in its juices. Set aside each batch of meat on a plate.

3 When all the meat is cooked, return it to the pan. Add the flour and stir well. Add the Madeira or sherry and stir vigorously to blend it with the meat juices and give a smooth thick mixture, then stir in the red wine, beef stock and mustard.

4 Bring to the boil, check the seasoning, reduce the heat and return the onion mixture to the pan along with the mushrooms, chestnuts, bay leaves and thyme. Simmer, covered, for 1 hour, stirring occasionally until the meat is tender. Taste and adjust the seasoning if needed. Remove the bay leaves and thyme sprigs. Remove from the heat and allow to cool completely.

5 Preheat the oven to 220°C/200°C fan/Gas 7. Spoon the filling mixture into the pie dish. Roll out the pastry to a rectangle a little larger than the top of the dish. Cut a 1cm- (½in-) strip off

Continues overleaf

the edge of the pastry and place it around the rim of the pie dish. Dampen this with water, then lay the pastry lid on top. Press the edges well to seal then trim the edge with a sharp knife. Using the blade of the knife, make little cuts all around the cut edge of the pastry to help it rise evenly, then crimp the edges. Make a hole in the centre of the pie for the steam to escape. If you wish roll out the remaining pastry trimmings and cut a few diamond-shaped leaves. Score the veins with a knife then arrange the leaves on top of the pie.

6 Brush the pie all over with the beaten egg (try not to let it drip down the sides of the pastry as this will prevent it rising). Bake the pie for about 35–45 minutes, until golden, risen and the filling is piping hot.

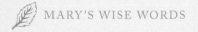 MARY'S WISE WORDS   *Venison is available in good supermarkets and butchers in the autumn and winter. Look for stewing venison – shoulder meat is ideal.*

ASIAN BELLY OF PORK WITH *Stir-fried* VEGETABLES

SERVES 6

PREPARE AHEAD
Cook the pork for the first 3 hours, but do not increase the oven temperature at the end. Cool the pork completely then cut into very thick slices and chill. To reheat, cook at 220°C/200°C fan/Gas 7 for 20–30 minutes, wrapped in foil. The vegetables should be cooked at the last minute but can be sliced ahead of time and kept in plastic bags in the fridge ready to be cooked.

1 x 1.5kg (3lb) piece of boned belly of pork, scored finely

2 teaspoons salt

4 tablespoons soy sauce

3 tablespoons clear honey

a 2cm (¾ in) knob of fresh root ginger, grated

100ml (3½fl oz) orange juice

200ml (7fl oz) water

1 teaspoon Chinese five-spice powder

1 tablespoon cornflour

200ml (7fl oz) chicken stock

This delicious roast has an oriental flavour that is perfect to serve with stir-fried vegetables, and is great for a smart supper as it can be prepared well in advance.

When preparing the pork, make sure the belly of pork skin is scored as finely as possible so that it crisps up well and is easy to break into pieces. The crackling is everybody's favourite part of roast pork, and this will be no exception, so make sure you distribute it evenly between your guests when serving.

1 Preheat the oven to 150°C/130°C fan/Gas 2.

2 Rub salt into the scored skin of the pork belly. Mix together the soy, honey, ginger, orange juice, water and five-spice together and pour into a small roasting tin. Sit the pork on top.

3 Cook in the oven for 3 hours until completely tender then remove from the oven and set aside while you prepare the sauce.

4 To make the sauce, pour the juices from the pan into a jug. Skim off the fat then pour into a small pan. Mix the cornflour with a little cold water to make a smooth paste, then add to the pan along with the stock. Stir over a high heat until thickened slightly. Set aside then reheat just before serving.

5 Increase the oven temperature to 220°C/200°C fan/Gas 7. Line the roasting tin with foil, put the pork on top and fold up the sides of the foil to cover the sides, but not the top of the meat. Roast in the oven for 20–30 minutes until the skin is crisp and brown.

Continues overleaf

4 Add the lardons and shallots to the frying pan along with the remaining butter, and fry for 5 minutes until the onions are tender and lightly golden.

5 Measure the flour into a bowl. Whisk in the sherry or wine, whisking until you have a smooth consistency. Add the reserved mushroom liquid and the chicken stock.

6 Pour the liquid into the frying pan and stir until thickened and smooth. Add the thyme, porcini mushrooms, chestnut mushrooms and all of the guinea fowl pieces except the breasts. Season and bring to the boil.

7 Remove the guinea fowl from the heat and cover. Transfer into the oven and cook for 20–25 minutes, until nearly tender. Add the breasts and continue to cook in the oven for a further 10–15 minutes.

8 Stir in the crème fraîche and sprinkle with parsley. Just before serving, cut the breasts in half so that everyone gets a bit of breast and dark meat.

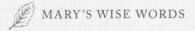 MARY'S WISE WORDS

You could snip the knuckle off the drumstick with kitchen shears, so that they look a little smarter. It is also a good idea to cut off the gristly sinew at the knuckle end of the drumsticks when cooked.

If preferred, roast the birds whole then joint and remove the skin. The meat will not have the browned appearance, so add it to the sauce and reheat together as a casserole.

SALMON EN CROÛTE WITH *Pesto-Roasted* VEGETABLES

SERVES 10

PREPARE AHEAD

Make the 'parcel' but do not bake, and keep in the fridge for up to 1 day. Cook as in step 6, on a preheated tray.

FREEZE

Wrap the uncooked 'parcel' in foil, then put in a plastic bag and seal. Freeze for up to 1 month. Thaw for about 12 hours in the fridge before baking as in step 6.

3 red peppers, halved and deseeded

2 red onions, cut into eight wedges

3 courgettes, cut lengthways into 1cm slices

3 tablespoons olive oil

2 x 320g packs ready-rolled puff pastry

1 x 1kg (2lb 2oz) side of salmon, skin removed, cut from the centre

3 tablespoons sun-dried tomato pesto

1 egg, beaten

FOR THE SAUCE

600ml (1 pint) pouring double cream

juice of 1 lemon

4 tablespoons sun-dried tomato pesto

4 tablespoons chopped basil

A dinner party and summer buffet classic, this wonderful dish has stood the test of time because it never fails to look impressive and is so easy to prepare ahead and to serve. Different recipes have cropped up in my books over the years but I make no apology for that as I don't think you can ever have too many. With its sun-dried tomato pesto, basil and roasted peppers and courgettes, this version brings a taste of the Mediterranean to one of the most British of dishes. Just add new potatoes and a side salad. I prefer to serve it hot, but it can be served at room temperature too.

1 Preheat the oven to 220°C/200°C fan/Gas 7.

2 Place the red peppers, onion and courgette in a large roasting tin with the olive oil and roast for 20–25 minutes, until the vegetables are charred and tender. Allow to cool, then peel and discard the skin from the red peppers and cut them into bite-sized pieces.

3 Place a large baking tray in the oven to heat.

4 Unroll one pack of pastry and roll it out to make it a little longer – about 2cm larger all around – than the piece of fish (check that it will fit on the baking tray – you may have to place it diagonally). Place the pastry on top of a sheet of baking paper so that you can easily slide the completed parcel on to the baking tray. Place the salmon in the centre of the pastry and spread with the pesto, top with the courgettes and onions and lay the red peppers on top. Brush the pastry around the fish with some of the beaten egg.

Continues overleaf

5 Roll out the other pack of pastry to a rectangle slightly larger than the first one so that it drapes over the fish and filling. Carefully lift it on to the salmon and vegetables, trim off any excess and press the edges down well to seal. Re-roll the pastry trimmings thinly and cut out pastry decorations if you like. Brush the pastry with more beaten egg.

6 Carefully slide the parcel on to the preheated baking tray (still on the parchment) and bake for 35–40 minutes, until golden brown, both on top and underneath. Allow to rest for 10 minutes while you make the sauce.

7 To make the sauce, gently heat the cream, and stir in the lemon juice and pesto. Remove from the heat then stir in the basil just before serving.

8 Serve the salmon en croute, cut into slices, with the sauce in a jug alongside.

 MARY'S WISE WORDS   *Try to buy a wide piece of fish rather than a long thin fillet, as it will fit in the oven better. It is also essential to heat the baking tray in the oven first, as this instantly starts to cook the pastry, preventing a soggy bottom!*

Use basil pesto if you prefer.

A WINTER BUFFET

MAIN COURSE

Salmon en Croûte with
Pesto-Roasted Vegetables

Rich Beef and Mushroom Stew

Spiced Garden Vegetable Casserole

SIDE DISHES

Foolproof Green Salad

Mustard Mash

DESSERT

Jaffa Panacotta with Sliced Oranges

Meringue Tranche with
Summer Fruits and Cream

BAKED *Salted* SEA BASS

SERVES 4

4 small whole sea bass,
  scaled and gutted
2 lemons, thinly sliced
 a bunch of thyme
1kg (2lb 2oz) sea salt
freshly ground black pepper

**Sea bass is now so popular that it is an inexpensive fish to
serve for a dinner party. By cooking it in a crust of salt you
seal in all the moisture and sweetness of the fish, and guests
will be amazed to see you crack open the salt crust to reveal
the succulent fish.**

1 Preheat the oven to 220°C/200°C fan/Gas 7.

2 Season the fish with pepper and fill the cavities with lemon
slices and thyme sprigs.

3 Put the salt into a bowl, add 6 tablespoons of water and stir
until sludgy. Spread a thin layer (about 1cm thick) on to the
base of a roasting tin. Arrange the sea bass on top. Spread the
remaining salt mixture over the top and pat on to the fish to
make a crust.

4 Bake in the oven for 35–40 minutes. To test if the fish is
cooked, make a hole in the crust and using a small knife, peel
away the skin; the flesh should be opaque.

 MARY'S WISE WORDS   *You must use rock salt for this dish as fine salt will be too powdery and
won't form a crust.*

Spring CHICKEN WITH LEMON AND FENNEL

SERVES 6

PREPARE AHEAD

This can be made up to a day in advance, but it is best to add the cream when the casserole has been reheated.

1 fennel bulb, trimmed, cored and thinly sliced

400ml (12fl oz) chicken stock

2 tablespoons olive oil

a knob of butter

6 small skinless, boneless chicken breasts

2 garlic cloves, crushed

25g (1oz) plain flour

200ml (7fl oz) white wine

juice of 1 small lemon

1 tablespoon chopped thyme leaves

200ml (7fl oz) full-fat crème fraîche

salt and freshly ground black pepper

a small handful of parsley, to garnish (optional)

This is a very fresh-tasting, light and easy dish for a spring or summer supper party, that takes just 30 minutes to cook. Although you might think the slightly aniseed flavour of fennel would be overpowering, cooking the fennel until soft, as I do here, mellows the flavour and gives the dish a lovely sweetness too. It is great served with mashed or new potatoes, carrots and asparagus.

1 Place the fennel in a pan with half the stock, bring to the boil, then cover with a lid and simmer for 10 minutes until tender.

2 Heat the oil and butter in a large frying pan and when hot, fry the chicken for 3–4 minutes on each side until golden brown. You may need to do this in batches. Remove from the pan and set aside.

3 Add the garlic to the frying pan and fry for 30 seconds, then add the remaining stock. Bring to the boil.

4 Mix the flour with the white wine to make a paste. Add the paste to the boiling stock and whisk briskly to thicken. Return the chicken to the pan with the lemon juice, fennel and its liquid and the thyme leaves. Bring up to the boil and cover with a lid. Reduce the heat to a simmer and cook for about 15 minutes or until the chicken is tender. Taste and adjust the seasoning.

5 Stir the crème fraiche into the pan and serve sprinkled with plenty of parsley, if you wish.

 MARY'S WISE WORDS

I am always amazed at how I learn something new every day. I like my fennel to be really soft, so when testing this recipe we boiled it in wine first, and to our surprise the wine made the fennel very tough and stringy – so always cook it in stock or water!

DUCK BREASTS WITH
Mango CREAM SAUCE

SERVES 6

PREPARE AHEAD

The onions and duck can be prepared and chilled for a few hours before assembling and cooking the dish.

2 tablespoons vegetable oil

1 large onion, finely chopped

6 small duck breasts, skin removed (see Mary's Wise Words)

3 tablespoons mango chutney

3 tablespoons Worcestershire sauce

300ml (½ pint) pouring double cream

1 teaspoon paprika

salt and freshly ground black pepper

a little chopped parsley, to garnish

You might not think of serving duck in a rich sauce, but by removing the skin the meat itself is less rich. This sauce is so quick to make and complements the duck beautifully. Its intriguing flavour will have everyone guessing what it is made from. Just serve the duck with mashed potatoes and a green vegetable, and be prepared to share the recipe with your guests!

1 Preheat the oven to 200°C/180°C fan/Gas 6.

2 Heat 1 tablespoon of the oil in a large frying pan and fry the onion over a low heat until soft and transparent.

3 Spoon the onion into a shallow baking dish (something that will hold all the duck breasts comfortably with a little space between them).

4 Add the remaining oil to the frying pan and when hot, add the duck breasts and fry for 2 minutes on each side until golden brown. Place the duck on top of the onion and season well.

5 Mix together the mango chutney, Worcestershire sauce and cream, then season and pour over the duck.

6 Place in the oven and cook for 10 minutes. Stir well, then sprinkle with paprika and cook for a further 15 minutes, until the duck is tender but still slightly pink in the centre. Remove from the oven and leave to rest for 10 minutes before serving. Garnish with the chopped parsley.

 MARY'S WISE WORDS

To remove the duck skin, pull the skin away from the meat – most of it comes away easily but if necessary slide a knife between the skin and meat to loosen the sinews.

Pistachio BASIL PESTO WITH *Fettuccine*

SERVES 4

PREPARE AHEAD
The pesto can be made
1–2 days in advance and
kept in the fridge.

1 x 80g pack basil leaves

½ teaspoon caster sugar

100g (4oz) shelled
pistachio nuts

100g (4oz) Parmesan cheese,
grated, plus extra to serve

2 garlic cloves, sliced in half

150ml (¼ pint) olive oil

350g (12oz) fettuccine pasta

100ml (4fl oz) pouring
double cream

salt and freshly ground
black pepper

This pasta dish is rich, creamy and a bit more unusual than the usual basil pesto. I have a great trick for keeping your homemade pesto bright green: just blanch the basil as below, it makes the pesto looks stunning when brought to the table.

1 Blanch 50g (2oz) of the basil leaves in boiling water for 1 minute. Drain in a sieve, then run cold water over the leaves and drain well.

2 Put the blanched basil, sugar, nuts, Parmesan and garlic into a food processor. Whizz until roughly chopped. Pour in the oil and 50ml (2 fl oz) of cold water. Whizz until smooth then season to taste. Chop the remaining 30g (1oz) of basil.

3 Cook the pasta in boiling salted water according to the packet instructions, reserving 100ml (4fl oz) of the cooking water before draining.

4 Put the puréed basil mixture into the saucepan along with the cream and bring up to the boil. Add the pasta, chopped basil and reserved pasta water, toss together and season. Serve at once with extra grated Parmesan.

 MARY'S WISE WORDS

Use penne pasta if preferred. If you wish, add 100g (4oz) peeled prawns along with the cream.

If time is short, you can always use a carton of fresh pesto, which is available in the best supermarkets.

"Just blanch the basil, and your pesto will keep its stunning bright green colour"

A Classic Roast

A CLASSIC ROAST

This chapter is all about the classic definition of a 'roast' – a joint of meat that is roasted in the oven and most often served up as Sunday lunch. But in an age when many of us are trying to reduce the quantity of meat we consume, I wanted to include a different style of Sunday lunch too, and I thought a luxurious fish pie would fit the bill (page 191). Like a roast, it's easily prepared ahead of time, then popped in the oven for you to forget about, so you can enjoy time with your guests.

Roasts needn't be simply about the meat. I've included different ways of preparing each type of joint so that you can pack in lots of additional flavour. A lamb rack is served with a delicious herb and mustardy breadcrumb crust (page 172); gammon is covered in a sticky but not too sweet maple-syrup glaze and is served with a spicy homemade chutney (page 186); while chicken gets a traybake treatment and is paired with lots of wonderful Mediterranean flavours, such as olives and preserved lemons (page 192).

And of course, roast lunch wouldn't be complete without Roast Potatoes (page 176), Yorkshire Puddings (page 182) and a generous selection of vegetables to dive into (page 178). I've my top tips for achieving that crisp golden crust and soft, fluffy interior to your potatoes as well as perfectly-risen Yorkshire puds.

Finally, my Sunday lunch has to end with a homemade pudding, and I'd urge you turn to the Cold Desserts and Hot Puddings chapters (pages 214 and 251) to choose a sweet finish to yours.

Vegetable PLATTER

SERVES 10

750g (1¾lb) peeled sweet
potatoes, cut into 2cm
(1in) cubes

350g (12oz) baby carrots,
scrubbed and cut in half
lengthways with green tops

50g (2oz) butter, melted, plus
extra for greasing the dish

450g (1lb) red cabbage,
finely shredded

4 tablespoons light
muscovado sugar

4 tablespoons white
wine vinegar

350g (12oz) frozen petit pois

I love to serve a lot of interesting vegetables at a dinner party, but don't want to be cooking them at the last minute. So I always get a platter cooked and ready to reheat at the last minute, just as they do in restaurants.

1 Bring a large pan of salted water to the boil. Add the sweet potato cubes, bring back to the boil and cook for 2 minutes. Add the carrots to the pan with the potato and cook both vegetables together for a further 6 minutes or until just tender when pierced with a knife. Drain then refresh with cold water to stop the cooking process. Return to the pan and toss with half the melted butter so that it coats the hot vegetables.

2 Heat the remaining melted butter in a large saucepan, add the cabbage, sugar and vinegar. Stir over a low heat, cover and simmer for 30 minutes until tender. Season to taste then leave to cool.

3 Cook the petit pois in a pan of boiling water for 2 minutes. Drain, cover with cold water and drain again.

4 Butter a large, flat ovenproof dish. Arrange the vegetables in four rows (sweet potatoes and carrots at the ends) and season with salt and pepper. Cover with a piece of buttered foil and chill until ready to reheat.

5 To reheat, preheat the oven to 220°C/200°C fan/Gas 7. Cook, covered in foil, for 25 minutes, checking them after 20 minutes, until all the vegetables are steaming hot.

 MARY'S WISE WORDS

Whatever vegetables you wish to cook, make sure they still have a little bite before you cool then reheat them. You could also use sugarsnap peas or mangetout, baby carrots, mixed broad beans and peas, and tiny boiled new potatoes.

Don't over-heat the vegetables, otherwise they will lose their colour, and don't keep them hot in the oven once reheated for the same reason.

A SUNDAY ROAST

MAIN COURSE

*Slow-roast Shoulder of Lamb
with Rosemary and Paprika Rub*

SIDE DISHES

Fennel and Potato Gratin

Roast Potatoes

Yorkshire Puddings

DESSERT

Plum and Marzipan Tarte Tatin

"Sunday lunch wouldn't be complete without roast potatoes and a generous selection of vegetables to dive into"

Three Fish PIE WITH *Leeks* AND WHITE WINE

SERVES 6

PREPARE AHEAD

The pie can be assembled and chilled in the fridge for up to 12 hours before cooking.

FREEZE

Make the pie but omit the eggs as they become tough and rubbery when frozen. You can freeze the cooked pie for up to 1 month. Reheat in the oven at 200°C/180°C fan/ Gas 6 for about 45 minutes.

FOR THE TOPPING

1kg (2lb 2oz) potatoes, peeled and cut into large chunks

a knob of butter

a little milk

50g (2oz) Gruyère cheese, grated

salt and freshly ground black pepper

FOR THE FILLING

75g (3oz) butter

2 leeks, sliced

75g (3oz) plain flour

150ml (¼ pint) white wine

600ml (1 pint) milk

2 tablespoons chopped parsley

750g (1¾lb) mixture of salmon, smoked haddock and fresh haddock fillet, skinned and cut into cubes

6 eggs, hard-boiled, peeled and quartered

The leeks and wine make this fish pie taste a little more sophisticated than traditional versions so you could confidently serve it at a casual supper party. If cooking for children you can replace the white wine quantity with more milk.

1 You will need a 2.25 litre (4 pint) ovenproof dish. Preheat the oven to 200°C/180°C fan/Gas 6.

2 Put the potatoes into a saucepan of cold salted water. Bring up to the boil and simmer until completely tender, about 20 minutes. Drain well then mash with the butter and milk. Add pepper and check the seasoning.

3 To make the fish filling, melt the butter in a saucepan, add the leeks and stir over the heat, cover with a lid and simmer gently for 10 minutes until soft.

4 Measure the flour into a small bowl. Add the wine and whisk together until smooth. Add the milk to the leeks, bring to the boil then add the wine mixture. Stir briskly until thickened. Season and add the parsley and fish. Stir over the heat for 2 minutes then spoon into the dish. Scatter over the eggs. Allow to cool until firm.

5 Spoon the mashed potatoes over the fish mixture and mark with a fork. Sprinkle with the cheese. Bake for 35–40 minutes until lightly golden on top and bubbling around the edges.

 MARY'S WISE WORDS

You can of course use just haddock, cod or salmon, or add a few prawns and some mussels too, if you prefer. You could also make the sauce with cider instead of wine. I sometimes add some spinach or peas to the mixture too.

Mediterranean ALL-IN-ONE CHICKEN

SERVES 6

1kg (2lb 2oz) main crop
  potatoes, peeled and cut
  into 5cm (2in) chunks

3 tablespoons olive oil

1 large onion, cut into wedges

2 garlic cloves, crushed

6 rashers of smoked streaky
  bacon, snipped into 1cm
  (½ in) pieces

6 chicken thighs

6 chicken drumsticks

5 preserved lemons,
  cut into quarters

1½ teaspoons paprika

3 courgettes, thickly sliced

1 x 200g can anchovy-stuffed
  green olives, drained

salt and freshly ground
  black pepper

This is a great way to feed the family as the chicken and veg are all cooked in one very large tray in the oven. It takes only minutes to put everything together then it sits in the oven for under an hour with no fussy finishing off to do and only one pan to wash up. The recipe allows one chicken thigh and one drumstick per person, but use less if you are not such big eaters.

I love stuffed olives, but use plain green or black ones if you prefer. The preserved lemons really give a lovely citrus tang to the dish and are well worth using but if you can't find them use one sliced lemon instead.

1 Preheat the oven to 220°C/200°C fan/Gas 7.

2 Place the potatoes in a large roasting tin with 2 tablespoons of the oil. Toss well to coat them. Add the onion, garlic, bacon and chicken pieces and toss together.

3 Add the lemons to the roasting tin. Season everything well and sprinkle with the paprika. Roast for 40 minutes.

4 In a bowl toss the courgettes in the remaining tablespoon of oil and season with salt and pepper, then poke them in among the chicken and scatter the olives over the top. Return to the oven for a further 20 minutes, until the chicken and vegetables are golden brown and tender.

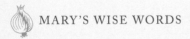 MARY'S WISE WORDS

Don't overcrowd the roasting tin, you need everything to be in a single layer or it will not cook evenly – divide between 2 tins if necessary.

Preserved lemons can usually be bought in jars in the speciality section of the supermarket. Traditionally from Morocco, the lemons are preserved in salt water and are beautifully soft and citrusy. Use them to flavour tagines and chicken or pork dishes. They will keep in the jar in the fridge for 1 month, or you can freeze them in a freezer-proof container for up to 3 months.

Vegetables, Salads and Sides

VEGETABLES, SALADS
AND SIDES

I fear that vegetables are often the poor relation of the dinner party.
So often we concentrate on the main course and pud and the vegetables
are an afterthought. But I love salads, both as part of a main course and
to serve on their own as a light lunch. The Broad Bean and Little Gem
Salad (page 198) is delicious and is a bit like a Caesar salad, perfect for
lunchtime in the sun.

I wanted to include more substantial salads based on rice and couscous,
too, so my Fiery Red Rice and Carrot Salad (page 208) is made with
nutty, sweet Camargue rice, which is something that I now keep in my
store cupboard as it makes such a colourful addition to a buffet table.

Couscous is also a great store cupboard ingredient as it takes only minutes
to soak and turn into a tasty meal with lots of vegetables. Just make sure you
season it well. I am always surprised at how much flavouring coucous soaks
up, so the more seasoning you add, the tastier it will be.

BROAD BEAN AND *Little Gem* SALAD

SERVES 10

PREPARE AHEAD
The dressing can be made up
to 3 days in advance.

300g (10oz) frozen
baby broad beans

6 Little Gem lettuces

100g (4oz) Parmesan
cheese, or vegetarian hard
cheese, cut into shavings
with a potato peeler

salt and freshly ground
black pepper

FOR THE CROUTONS

5 thick slices of white
bread, crusts removed,
cut into cubes

6 tablespoons olive oil

FOR THE MUSTARD
DRESSING

3 tablespoons Dijon mustard

5 tablespoons white
wine vinegar

8 tablespoons olive oil

5 tablespoons double
or single cream

1 tablespoon caster sugar

This is such a lovely, fresh-tasting salad, ideal for an al fresco meal. If you want to include meat in this dish, you could add six fried, crispy, crumbled bacon rashers.

1 First make the croutons. Preheat the oven to 200°C/180°C fan/Gas 6. Place the cubes of bread in a plastic bag, pour in the oil and season well. Pick up the bag to toss the cubes in the oil so that they are evenly coated. Spread the bread out in a single layer on a baking tray and cook in the oven until browned – about 5 minutes. Watch them all the time to prevent scorching, and shake them occasionally to make sure they brown evenly.

2 Cook the broad beans in boiling water for about 3–4 minutes until tender, then drain and refresh in cold water. Remove the beans from their skins and set aside.

3 Trim the very ends off of the lettuces but keep the root intact, then cut each lettuce into six wedges. Arrange on a serving platter, scatter over the beans, Parmesan and croutons and season with salt and pepper.

4 Measure all the dressing ingredients into a large bowl, whisk until smooth and season. Pour the dressing over the salad, then toss everything together.

 MARY'S WISE WORDS

If serving vegetarians look for Parmesan-style cheese made without animal rennet.

Do not salt the water when boiling the broad beans – salt will toughen them.

Foolproof GREEN SALAD WITH DILL DRESSING

SERVES 10

8 spring onions, finely sliced

8 celery sticks, finely sliced

1 small fennel bulb,
  finely sliced

1 romaine lettuce

½ large cucumber, halved
  lengthways and thickly sliced

200g pack mixed salad leaves

100g pack rocket or watercress

FOR THE DILL DRESSING

9 tablespoons extra virgin
  olive oil

3 tablespoons white
  wine vinegar

1 tablespoon balsamic vinegar

1 tablespoon Dijon mustard

1 tablespoon caster sugar

a bunch of chopped dill

salt and freshly ground
  black pepper

I like to add some crunchy vegetables to my green salad to liven it up. And if you want to prepare this salad ahead so that the lettuce doesn't wilt, the trick is simple – just don't toss it with the dressing until ready to serve.

1 First, make the dill dressing. Whisk together the oil, white wine and balsamic vinegars, mustard, sugar and some salt and pepper in a bowl until evenly combined and thickened. Taste and season accordingly then add the dill.

2 Place the spring onions, celery and fennel in a large salad bowl. Add the dressing and mix well. Tear the romaine lettuce into manageable pieces. Place the cucumber and the romaine leaves in the bowl on top of the fennel. Season then top with the mixed leaves and rocket or watercress. Chill for up to 4 hours.

3 Just before serving toss everything together.

MARY'S WISE WORDS

Don't toss the salad until ready to serve, as the dressing will soften the leaves. The dressing can be chilled in the fridge for up to a week in a screw top jar. Just give it a good shake before using and add the dill only just before serving. Use the highest quality olive oil for the best flavour.

"Don't toss salad until ready to serve,
as the dressing will soften the leaves"

ROASTED *Fennel*, ONION AND POTATO WITH *Parmesan* TOPPING

3 large fennel bulbs

600g (1lb 6oz) large potatoes, peeled

3 onions, each cut into 6 wedges

50g (2oz) butter, plus extra for greasing

2 garlic cloves, crushed

50g (2oz) Parmesan cheese, grated

This simple side – a hearty combination of potatoes and vegetables – is all cooked in one dish so it's perfect for a dinner party or Sunday lunch. In fact, it is so tasty you could eat it as a supper on its own, served with a green vegetable or lightly dressed salad.

1 Preheat the oven to 200°C/180°C fan/Gas 6. Butter a shallow 2.5-litre (4-pint) ovenproof dish, about 23 x 30cm (9 x 12in).

2 Trim the tops from the fennel and cut each bulb in half through the root, then cut each in half lengthways into three wedges. Cut the potatoes into wedges the same size as the fennel wedges.

3 Bring a large pan of salted water to the boil, then cook the fennel and onion for about 5 minutes. Add the potatoes and boil for a further 5 minutes, until all the vegetables are just tender. Drain well.

4 Put the butter and the garlic in the empty vegetable pan and set over a low heat until just melted. Add the vegetables to the butter, toss until coated, then tip into the prepared dish. Sprinkle with the Parmesan. Bake for 30–40 minutes, until piping hot.

 MARY'S WISE WORDS

It is essential to pre-cook the potatoes and fennel, otherwise they absorb too much butter and you would have to use more, giving an over-rich result; the fennel would also be much tougher.

Jewelled COUSCOUS SALAD

SERVES 6

PREPARE AHEAD

The salad can be made, without the broccoli, up to 3 days ahead and kept in the fridge. Add the broccoli no more than 1 hour before serving, otherwise it will lose its colour when the dressing is added.

250g (9oz) couscous

2 lemons

150g (5oz) Tenderstem broccoli

100g (4oz) ready-to-eat dried apricots

seeds of 1 pomegranate

2 tablespoons chopped parsley

6 drops of Tabasco sauce

2 tablespoons light olive oil

salt and freshly ground black pepper

This versatile salad is delicious on its own, or you can serve it with grilled chicken or lamb or with flakes of smoked trout or mackerel. Vary it by adding flaked almonds instead of seeds, or dried cranberries instead of pomegranates. Fresh mint or coriander leaves are also very tasty – just use whatever you have.

1 Place the couscous in a bowl. Grate the zest of one of the lemons and add it to the couscous along with the juice of both lemons. Add 350ml (12fl oz) boiling water and plenty of seasoning. Leave to soak until all the water has been absorbed.

2 Cut the broccoli into 5cm (2in) lengths and cook in boiling water for 3 minutes. Drain and plunge into cold water to stop it cooking. Drain well and add to the couscous.

3 Snip the apricots into very small pieces using kitchen scissors, then add to the couscous along with the pomegranate seeds and parsley. Add the Tabasco and olive oil and check the seasoning.

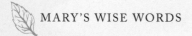 **MARY'S WISE WORDS** *Tabasco sauce is made from hot chillies so use it sparingly. If you don't have any, use a little chopped red chilli or even a little sweet chilli sauce. A little harissa paste is also delicious stirred through.*

Goat's Cheese, POMEGRANATE AND ONION SALAD WITH *Balsamic Dressing*

SERVES 6

PREPARE AHEAD
Cook the onion up to
2 days in advance and
keep in the fridge.

1 tablespoon olive oil

2 onions, sliced

1 tablespoon light
muscovado sugar

100g (4oz) lamb's lettuce

150g (5oz) firm goat's cheese,
broken into pieces

100g (4oz) pomegranate seeds
(roughly 1 pomegranate)

salt and freshly ground
black pepper

FOR THE DRESSING

2 tablespoons balsamic vinegar

4 tablespoons olive oil

½ teaspoon Dijon mustard

1 teaspoon soy sauce

A lovely light salad bursting with colour and contrasting textures and flavours. The sweetness of the caramelised onions is balanced by the juicy sweet-and-sourness of pomegranates and the tangy, salty flavour of the goat's cheese.

1 Heat the oil in a frying pan. Add the onions and fry for 2 minutes. Cover with a lid and simmer gently for 5 minutes until soft. Add the sugar and stir until caramelised. Remove from the heat and leave to cool.

2 Mix all of the dressing ingredients together in a jug.

3 Arrange the lamb's lettuce on six small plates. Scatter over the goat's cheese, pomegranate seeds and onions. Season the salad portions then drizzle over the dressing.

MARY'S WISE WORDS

Make sure you use a firm goat's cheese that will crumble easily, rather than a soft, creamy one.

To remove the seeds from a pomegranate, cut it in half. Place each half cut-side down on a worktop and bash the skin with a rolling pin to release the seeds, then turn the right way up and break the skin, and the seeds will fall out easily.

CRUNCHY *Broccoli* SALAD

SERVES 6

450g (1lb) broccoli (about
   2 heads), stalks discarded and
   cut into tiny florets

8 spring onions, finely chopped

2 tablespoons white
   wine vinegar

3 tablespoons caster sugar

200ml (7fl oz) mayonnaise

My cousin Robin gave me this simple recipe, and I like to serve it as part of a buffet. The raw, crunchy broccoli makes a lovely textural contrast when served with a mixed plate of cold meat and salads.

1 Place the broccoli florets in a non-metallic bowl with the remaining ingredients. Refridgerate overnight and serve chilled.

Lime COLESLAW

SERVES 6

PREPARE AHEAD

This can be made up to
   2 days in advance and
   kept in the fridge.

1 small white cabbage, about
   450g (1lb), finely shredded

200g (7oz) carrots,
   coarsely grated

a bunch of spring onions,
   finely sliced

grated zest and juice of 1 lime

200ml (7fl oz) mayonnaise

4 tablespoons chopped
   coriander leaves

Coleslaw is always a popular addition to a summer table. This recipe is a variation of the classic as I have added lime juice and coriander for a change. It is delicious served on top of my Pork and Red Pepper Burgers (page 118) or with the Maple-Glazed Gammon (page 186) or Spinach, Gruyère and Ham Quiche (page 124).

1 Mix the cabbage and carrots with the remaining ingredients and chill until ready to serve.

MARY'S WISE WORDS

Turn this into traditional coleslaw by mixing the only cabbage and carrots with the mayonnaise, or why not add a little curry paste and some raisins for another tasty variation?

Cold
Desserts

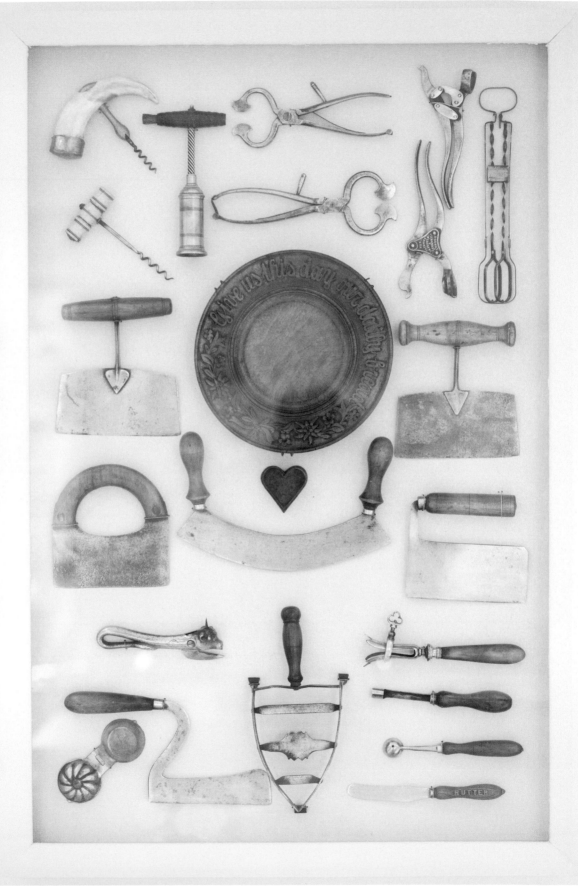

COLD DESSERTS

While hot desserts provide the warming, comforting and often heartier end to the type of meal we generally crave in the winter, cold desserts really come into their own in the warmer months and by early April we're generally looking for lighter finishes, perhaps to make use of the fruit that is coming into season.

In summer, when the garden is groaning with raspberries, loganberries, blackcurrants and redcurrants, I make summer puddings to freeze and enjoy later in the year. If you ever visit a pick-your-own farm and buy too much fruit, remember that it freezes beautifully too, so put it into freezer-proof bags or containers and keep it for summer puddings or red fruit salads. Or why not showcase them in my Summer Glory Trifle Cake (page 247) and Rosé Wine Jellies (page 232)?

And there's no reason why we shouldn't indulge in a bit of richness in the summer too. Cheesecakes are great favourites, and who doesn't love a slice of millionaire's shortbread? So I have combined the flavours of the two to make a wickedly good Millionaire's Cheesecake (page 221).

Meringues are a perfect partner for fruit and cream, so try the Meringue Tranche (page 244). It is perfect for a buffet and at almost 60cm (24in) long it looks spectacular laid down the centre of the table. Everyone will wonder how it fitted in the oven.

Finally, cold desserts also have a great advantage in that most can be prepared in advance and often frozen, too.

JAFFA *Panna Cotta*
WITH SLICED ORANGES

SERVES 10

PREPARE AHEAD
You can make this up to
  2 days in advance and
  store it in the fridge.
  Not suitable for freezing.

1 litre (1¾ pints) pouring
  double cream

200g (7oz) dark chocolate
  (50 per cent cocoa solids),
  finely chopped

7 oranges

100g (4oz) caster sugar

4 leaves of platinum grade
  gelatine, or 8 leaves of
  regular gelatine (see page 223)

a little vegetable oil,
  for greasing

This velvety, creamy chocolate dessert is almost nicer than chocolate mousse, which I find is often too rich or can be a worry if it contains raw egg white. And in this version, the chocolate is also beautifully complemented by some fresh orange slices. Best of all it is simple to make and is ideal for dinner parties as it will happily sit in the fridge for two days. If you don't want to make as many as ten, you can halve the mixture and it will serve six.

1 Very lightly oil ten individual 150ml (¼-pint) pudding basins or ramekins.

2 Heat the double cream in a small pan until it comes to the boil, then remove from the heat, stir in the chocolate and keep stirring until the chocolate has completely melted.

3 Grate the zest of four of the oranges and add to the chocolate cream. Squeeze the juice from two and add eight tablespoons of the juice to the chocolate mixture along with the sugar.

4 Place the gelatine in a little cold water and leave to soak for 10 minutes. When softened, remove the gelatine from the water, shake off excess water and place in the warm chocolate mixture. Stir until dissolved.

5 Strain the mixture through a sieve then divide equally between the oiled dishes. Place in the fridge and allow the panna cottas to set overnight or for at least 6 hours.

Continues overleaf

4 To make the cheesecake mixture, place the reserved caramel back into the pan that you cooked it in, and add 100ml (4fl oz) double cream. Place over a very low heat and stir until the caramel has dissolved.

5 Place the gelatine in 4 tablespoons of cold water and leave for 10 minutes to soften. Remove from the water, shake off any excess, and stir into the hot cream and caramel until dissolved.

6 Beat the remaining cream and cream cheese together until smooth, then stir in the cream and caramel mixture. Pour this over the caramel in the cake tin and leave for 2 hours until set.

7 To make the topping, warm the cream in a small pan until hot but not boiling. Add the chocolate and stir until melted and smooth. Allow to cool a little so that it will not melt the cheesecake. Pour over the cheesecake and leave to set in the fridge for at least 2 hours, ideally for 6 hours or until everything is set and firm. Serve cut into thin slices.

A NOTE ON GELATINE

Leaf gelatine is now more available than powdered, and gives a lovely smooth set. It is easy to use: just soften it in cold water for about 10 minutes, then drain, add to warm liquids (fruit juice, wine, liqueurs, warmed cream or milk) and watch it dissolve. However the strength of the setting power of gelatine varies depending on the brand you buy. Platinum grade gelatine uses 5 leaves of gelatine to set 600ml (1 pint). Some other gelatines use 12 leaves to set 600ml (1 pint).

If using cream cheese or double cream in a mixture you will not need as much gelatine, so follow the instructions on the back of the packet.In this recipe I have used half the amount of gelatine needed for 1 pint (i.e. 2½ leaves of platinum gelatine or 6 sheets of regular gelatine).

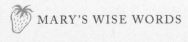 MARY'S WISE WORDS

It is important to cook the caramel until it thickens slightly so that it sets firm enough to cut. I find it best to set the timer and boil the mixture rapidly for 4–5 minutes, stirring all the time so that it does not burn on the base of the pan. You may find that the caramel will melt slightly where it meets the cheesecake, but this just makes it more delicious!

BRANDY SNAP *Raspberry* TIANS

The biscuits can be made up to a week in advance, wrapped in foil and kept in a cake tin until ready to serve. Assemble no more than 30 minutes before serving or the biscuits will soften.

25g (1oz) butter

25g (1oz) demerara sugar

25g (1oz) golden syrup

25g (1oz) plain flour

¼ teaspoon ground ginger

¼ teaspoon lemon juice

FOR THE FILLING

150ml (¼ pint) pouring double cream, whipped

150g (5oz) raspberries

a few mint leaves, to decorate

Tubular brandy snaps filled with cream are the classic way of serving the crunchy biscuits. This impressive-looking variation is simply a fun twist – small, flat brandy snap biscuits sandwiched together with cream and raspberries just before serving.

1 Preheat the oven to 160°C/140°C fan/Gas 3. Line two baking sheets with baking paper.

2 Measure the butter, sugar and syrup into a small pan and heat gently until the butter has melted and the sugar has dissolved and no longer feels grainy in the bottom of the pan. Leave the mixture to cool slightly then sift in the flour and ginger. Add the lemon juice and stir well to mix thoroughly. Place one level teaspoonful of mixture on a baking sheet in a neat circle. I find a little round measuring spoon helps to do this easily. Repeat, placing about 6 spoonfuls, well spaced apart on each sheet (you will need to bake them in batches).

3 Bake for about 8 minutes or until the mixture has spread out and is a dark golden colour. Ideally the biscuits will have spread to a circle about 5cm (2in) in diameter.

4 Remove from the oven. If the biscuits are too large or misshapen, use a biscuit or scone cutter to cut them into shape while still warm. Leave the brandy snaps to cool for a few minutes until firm enough to remove, and place on a wire rack or board to cool. Repeat with the remaining mixture.

5 To serve, spread a brandy snap with a little cream, top with raspberries and stack another biscuit on top. Add a little spoonful of cream and a raspberry on top. Decorate with mint leaves.

 MARY'S WISE WORDS *If the brandy snap mixture becomes too firm to spoon on to the baking sheet, roll it into tiny balls about the size of a 5p piece, or warm the mixture slightly.*

"I like to use seasonal flowers in low containers
to make the dining table look a little bit special"

SUMMER *Pudding* LOAF

SERVES 12

PREPARE AHEAD
This should be made a day in advance, but will also keep for 2 days in the fridge.

FREEZE
The pudding freezes beautifully. Just freeze in the tin, then when firm you can remove the tin and wrap in another layer of clingfilm to protect it. It will keep for months in the freezer and is a great way to enjoy summer berries all year long. Freeze any leftover fruit in a freezer bag. Defrost the loaf overnight in the fridge to ensure it is thoroughly defrosted.

butter, for greasing

1.5kg (3lb) mixed summer berries (such as blueberries, red- and blackcurrants, raspberries, blackberries and loganberries)

400g (14oz) caster sugar

1 large unsliced white tin loaf or use a loaf of thick-sliced white bread, ideally 2–3 days old

This loaf-shaped version of a summer pudding is easier to make than the traditional shape made in a pudding basin, and is also neater to slice and serve. If preferred, divide the recipe between two 450g (1lb) loaf tins, making one to serve now and one to freeze for later.

Remember, you will need to make this the day before you want to serve it as it needs overnight soaking.

1 Butter and line a 900g (2lb) loaf tin, or two 450g (1lb) tins, with a double layer of clingfilm.

2 Prepare the fruit by removing any leaves and stalks. Place blueberries, redcurrants and blackcurrants in a pan with the sugar and 75ml (3 fl oz) water and bring to the boil. Cook for 2–3 minutes until the berries have just softened and burst but don't overcook. You don't need to cook raspberries, blackberries or loganberries but if using only these types of berry, you will need to cook one type to get it to release its juice. If using in combination with the cooked fruit above, just add them to the pan at the end.

3 Using a sharp knife, cut the crusts off all sides of the loaf of bread, then cut the loaf lengthways into medium-thick slices so that you have long slices rather than square slices. Brush one side of the slices that are to line the tin generously with fruit juice from the berry mixture.

4 Place one slice of bread in the base of the tin, juice-brushed side down, trimming it to fit. Place a slice of bread either side of the inside of the tin and cut slices to fit both ends of the tin, putting the juice-brushed side against the tin.

Continues overleaf

A SUMMER BUFFET

SALADS

Broad Bean and
Little Gem Salad

Fiery Red Rice and Carrot Salad

MAINS

Maple-Glazed Gammon with Fresh
Apricot & Ginger Chutney

Roast Fillet of Beef wtih Roasted
Garlic & Mustard Cream

Salmon Tranches with Herb Sauce

DESSERT

Summer Pudding Loaf

Elderflower POSSET

SERVES 6

300ml (½ pint) pouring double cream

300ml (½ pint) undiluted elderflower cordial (ready-made or see page 242 for how to make your own)

summer berries such as strawberries, redcurrants or raspberries, to serve

a dusting of icing sugar, to decorate

This frozen dessert is so fragrant and so easy to make. The ingredients are just whipped together and put in the freezer, and it doesn't even need churning. Serve with summer berries for a light and refreshing end to a summer meal.

1 Place the cream in a mixing bowl and whip until it forms soft peaks, then gradually pour on the elderflower cordial, whisking until combined.

2 Freeze in pretty little dessert glasses or Martini glasses for at least 3 hours or overnight.

3 To serve, place in the fridge for 15–20 minutes to soften slightly, then put a few small strawberries, redcurrants or raspberries on each, decorate with a dusting of icing sugar and serve.

 MARY'S WISE WORDS *The posset can also be frozen in a freezer-proof container and scooped into glasses if you prefer. It could also be made with other fruit cordials, but don't be tempted to use fruit juice – it is the sugar in the cordial that makes the posset freeze smoothly.*

ELDERFLOWER *Cordial*

PREPARE AHEAD
The cordial will keep for
  2–3 months in the fridge

1.5kg (3lb) granulated sugar

1.5 litres (2½ pints) water

2 lemons

about 25 elderflower heads

50g (2oz) citric acid

2 Campden tablets

Elderflower cordial is fun to make if you have easy access to elderflower trees and the flowers that arrive in the early summer.

1 Measure the sugar and water into a large pan. Bring to the boil, stirring, until the sugar has dissolved. Remove from the heat and cool.

2 Slice the lemons thinly by hand or in a food processor. Put into a large plastic box or a bucket. Add the elderflower heads to the lemons along with the citric acid and Campden tablets. Pour over the cooled sugar syrup. Cover and leave overnight or for up to a couple of days.

3 Sieve and strain through muslin into sterilised bottles and store in the fridge. To serve, dilute to taste with still or fizzy water.

 MARY'S WISE WORDS

Look for elderflower heads from about the end of May; they can be frozen if you want to save them. Freeze about 25 heads in a bag and add to the hot sugar syrup straight from the freezer – this will stop them turning brown once defrosted. Cool the syrup before you add the remaining ingredients.

Campden tablets are used in home wine- and beer-making to kill bacteria and also to inhibit the growth of wild yeasts. Citric acid is a natural preservative and also gives a slightly sour flavour to the cordial. Look for both in pharmacists.

BRAMLEY *Apple* SORBET

SERVES 12

1kg (2lb 2oz) Bramley apples (about 5–6), peeled, cored and roughly chopped

100g (4oz) caster sugar

4 tablespoons golden syrup

4 tablespoons lemon juice

This is such an easy and cleansing dessert to serve in the autumn and winter after a heavy main course. At Christmas time I also sometimes serve it with some gently warmed leftover mincemeat.

1 Place the apples and sugar in a pan with 50ml (2fl oz) cold water. Cover with a lid and cook over a low heat for about 10 minutes, until the apples have collapsed almost to a purée. Mash them well with a fork. Remove from the heat and stir in the golden syrup and lemon juice.

2 Place the mixture in a shallow freezer-proof container and freeze for 2 hours until it has formed ice crystals around the edges. Stir well to break up the ice then return to the freezer and freeze until firm, stirring occasionally. If possible, churn in an ice-cream machine for a smoother consistency.

3 Remove from the freezer and place in the fridge 30 minutes before serving. Serve scooped or shaved into small glasses.

 MARY'S WISE WORDS *Serve this dessert with little shortbread biscuits or the Mini Brandy Snap Biscuits on page 224.*

SUMMER GLORY *Trifle* CAKE

SERVES 10–12

PREPARE AHEAD

Make the sponge 1–2 days in advance and keep loosely wrapped in clingfilm until needed. Once assembled, the dessert will keep in the fridge for 1 day.

FOR THE SPONGE

4 eggs

100g (4oz) caster sugar

100g (4oz) self-raising flour

FOR THE FILLING

5 tablespoons warmed, sieved raspberry or apricot jam

300g (10oz) raspberries

1 x 240g can apricots or peach slices in juice, drained and dried on kitchen paper

450ml (¾ pint) double cream

1 tablespoon medium sherry (optional)

1–2 tablespoons icing sugar

a few sprigs of mint, to decorate

This pretty dessert has all the flavours of a trifle – light sponge with jam, sherry flavoured cream and summer fruits – but is made into an easy-to-slice summer gateau. Use your favourite fruits, and omit the sherry if serving to children.

1 Line a 23 x 33cm (9 x 13in) Swiss roll tin with baking paper. Preheat the oven to 220°C/200°C fan/Gas 7.

2 Whisk the eggs and sugar together in a large bowl with an electric mixer until the mixture is light and fluffy, and has doubled in size, and the whisk leaves a trail when lifted out. Sift the flour on to the mixture, then using a large spoon, carefully fold it in until evenly mixed, taking care not to knock the air out of the mixture. Spoon the mixture into the prepared tin and give it a gentle shake so that it finds its own level and goes evenly into the corners.

3 Bake for about 10 minutes or until the sponge is pale golden brown and is beginning to shrink from the edges. Leave to cool in the tin for 10 minutes then turn out on to a cooling rack, peel off the baking paper and invert the cake so that it is the right way up again. Leave to cool completely.

4 Cut the edges off the cake then cut it lengthways into two equal pieces. Turn the cake upside down and spread both pieces with half the warm jam.

5 Place one piece of cake jam-side up on a serving plate. Arrange a row of raspberries down each long side of the cake and place a row in the centre. Reserve the remaining raspberries.

6 Slice the apricots, if using. Arrange most of the apricots or peaches between the rows of raspberries.

Continues overleaf

7 Whip the cream until it forms soft peaks. Stir in the sherry, if using, and icing sugar to taste. Spread a little cream on the bare side of the other length of cake and set aside. Spread the remaining cream on top of the fruit then place the other piece of cake on top, jam-side down.

8 Arrange the remaining raspberries and apricot or peach slices on top of the cake then brush with the remaining warmed jam and decorate with mint sprigs. If you like, you can chill the cake for up to 2 hours before serving.

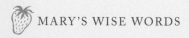 MARY'S WISE WORDS

Do not use fresh peaches unless serving within an hour or two as they will discolour.

You can of course use strawberries instead of raspberries, or why not make a chocolate sponge and fill with canned red cherries and cream? Just replace 25g (1oz) of the flour with cocoa powder.

If you accidentally over-whip the cream, fold a little milk into it to loosen it.

MANGO AND *Passion Fruit* TRIFLE

SERVES 6

PREPARE AHEAD
The trifle can be made
    up to 1 day ahead and
    kept in the fridge.

1 pack of trifle sponges
4 tablespoons apricot jam
juice of 2 oranges
3 tablespoons rum (optional)
2 ripe mangoes, diced
grated zest and juice of 1 lime
300g (11 oz) Greek yoghurt
2 tablespoons icing sugar
300ml (½ pint) double cream
3 passion fruits

As trifles can be made with just about any fruit you fancy, they can be served throughout the year. Many people think of them as a Christmassy dessert – the splendour of the dreamy cream, custard layers and sherry-soaked sponge bring a festive touch to the table. However, trifle is equally at home on a summer buffet table, where the fruit can take more of the centre-stage. This version offers a modern tropical twist on an old favourite.

I have soaked the trifle sponges in orange juice and rum, but you can omit the rum if serving to children.

1 You will need a 1.5-litre (3-pint) glass trifle dish or bowl. Cut the trifle sponges in half and spread the cut sides with the jam. Sandwich together and arrange in the base of the trifle dish. Pour the orange juice and rum, if using, over the sponges and leave to soak in.

2 Arrange half the diced mango on top of the sponges.

3 Stir the lime zest and juice into the yoghurt with 1 tablespoon of the icing sugar and spread on top of the mango.

4 Whip the double cream until it just holds its shape. Cut the passion fruits in half, scoop the seeds from 1½ fruits into the cream and stir in along with the remaining tablespoon of icing sugar. Spoon the cream on top of the yoghurt layer. Decorate with the remaining passion fruit and mango.

 MARY'S WISE WORDS   *Add a few blueberries or strawberries to the mango layer if you like. Why not top with some toasted coconut flakes too?*

Hot Puddings

HOT PUDDINGS

Classic, comforting British puddings, such as rice pudding (page 261), Queen of Puddings (page 264) and Sussex pond pudding (page 254) are often overlooked these days, which is sad as they are enthusiastically appreciated when they are served.

I believe in keeping our traditional dishes alive but I also believe in adapting recipes in order to suit your tastes or to improve the original if you can. So I have played with the old-fashioned Sussex pond pudding recipe, packing lots of chopped apple inside the suet crust and around the whole lemon so that the pudding doesn't collapse so much when cut and all those sweet buttery juices are set off against the sharpness of the apple and lemon. It is well worth making for a Sunday lunch as everyone will gasp with appreciation when the lovely golden suet crust is turned out of the pudding basin. It's wonderful served with a big jug of custard too.

My favourite dessert in this chapter is the Warm Chocolate Fondant Tart (page 266), which has a thin, very buttery pastry and slightly gooey chocolate centre; it cuts well and is perfect to serve for a dinner party. Or for a fruity end to a meal try my hot Plum and Marzipan Tarte Tatin (page 270) – its blushing red colour and sharp–sweet flavour is fabulous, and it is very simple to make as it uses ready-made puff pastry and marzipan.

In times when everyone is rushed and so often watching what they eat, a fabulous homemade pudding is a rare and special treat, so why not treat your friends and family soon?

Sussex POND PUDDING WITH APPLES

SERVES 6–8

PREPARE AHEAD
This pudding is best freshly
made although any leftovers
can be warmed up. Not
suitable for freezing.

FOR THE
SUET CRUST

225g (8oz) self-raising flour,
plus extra for dusting

100g (4oz) shredded suet

75ml (3fl oz) milk

FOR THE FILLING

4 Cox's apples, roughly
400g (14oz) in total,
peeled, cored and diced

150g (5oz) butter, cut into
cubes, plus extra for greasing

200g (7oz) light
muscovado sugar

1 large lemon

cream or custard, to serve

For anybody who isn't familiar with this traditional English delight, Sussex pond pudding is a classic basin pud, in which a soft layer of suet pastry encases a whole lemon and wonderful buttery juices. I love the traditional version but find that the whole thing always collapses when served so I thought it would be a good idea to pack the pudding with apples to bolster it – the result is even more delicious.

1 You will need a 1.5-litre (2½-pint) pudding basin. First make the suet crust. Measure the flour and suet into a bowl. Measure the milk into a jug, then add 75ml (3fl oz) cold water, to make 150ml (¼ pint) in total. Mix into the dry ingredients to make a soft dough.

2 Lightly dust the work surface with flour then roll out the dough to a 30cm (12in) circle. Cut a quarter out of the circle and set it aside to be used as the lid. Thickly butter the pudding basin, then line it with the pastry, pressing the join together.

3 Put the apples into a bowl with the butter and sugar, then place a little in the pudding basin on top of the suet pastry.

4 Prick the lemon all over with a cocktail stick then place in among the apples so that it sits upright. Pack as much of the remaining apples and butter mixture as you can around the lemon, piling it up to make a dome and packing it tightly down into the bowl.

5 Roll out the reserved suet pastry to make a circle to fit on top of the pudding and pinch the edges to seal.

Continues overleaf

6 Cut a square of foil and make a pleat in the centre. Place the foil over the pudding basin, tie with string then loop the string over the basin and under the string a couple of times to make a handle. Tie securely.

7 Place the lid of a jam jar in a large saucepan to stop the basin touching the bottom of the pan, add the pudding basin then pour boiling water around it so that it comes three quarters of the way up the sides. Cover the saucepan with a tight-fitting lid, and simmer for 3½ hours. Check the pan occasionally and top up with more boiling water as necessary.

8 To serve, remove the foil and invert the basin on to a plate. Remove the basin and serve the pudding with cream or custard. Expect the pudding to rapidly collapse – that is part of its charm!

 MARY'S WISE WORDS

I like to use parchment-lined foil as it is very thick and keeps the pudding well sealed when steaming.

Don't be tempted to use Bramley apples as they are too sharp and also they collapse when cooked.

If making this for vegetarians, use vegetable suet.

APPLE CRUMBLE WITH WALNUTS AND *Sunflower* SEEDS

PREPARE AHEAD

The crumble topping will keep well for a week in an airtight container and the apple will keep for 3–4 days in the fridge. Reheat the apple in a pan and top with the cold crumble mix – it does not reheat well.

FREEZE

Freeze the apple for up to 4 months (in individual portions if liked). Freeze the topping mixture in a freezer bag so you can sprinkle out as much as needed.

1.5kg (3lb) cooking apples, peeled, cored and thinly sliced

juice of ½ lemon

100g (4oz) light muscovado sugar

FOR THE TOPPING

50g (2oz) plain flour

50g (2oz) porridge oats

150g (5oz) light muscovado sugar

150g (5oz) walnuts, roughly chopped

50g (2oz) sunflower seeds

100g (4oz) softened butter

This is such a clever recipe: the apple and crumble are cooked separately, so not only does the crumble stay crisp, but also you can make it in advance and assemble the dessert whenever needed. The crumble topping is almost a granola and very tasty to nibble on, too.

1 Preheat the oven to 180°C/160°C fan/Gas 4.

2 Place the apples in a small flameproof casserole with the lemon juice, sugar and 6 tablespoons of water. Bring to the boil on the hob, then place in the oven and cook for about 20 minutes until the apple is tender but has not fallen to a pulp.

3 Weigh the topping ingredients into a mixing bowl and rub in the butter until it is evenly distributed and the mixture has formed small clumps. Spread the mixture evenly over a baking tray and bake for about 20 minutes until golden brown and crisp. Stir to break up the crumble and sprinkle over the hot apple.

 MARY'S WISE WORDS

You can cook the apples on the hob, but I find they break down into a pulp very quickly and that they keep their shape better if cooked in the oven. Use dessert apples if liked, but reduce the sugar to just a tablespoonful or so as they are much sweeter than cooking apples.

CLASSIC *Rice* PUDDING

SERVES 4

PREPARE AHEAD

Once baked, this will keep for two days in the fridge and can be warmed up in a pan or in the microwave before serving. It is also delicious served cold.

100g (4oz) short-grain pudding rice

50g (2oz) caster sugar

600ml (1 pint) milk

300ml (½ pint) single cream

freshly grated nutmeg

25g (1oz) butter

Not to be forgotten, rice pudding is one of the easiest, most inexpensive and, I think, most delicious puddings you can serve.

1 You will need a shallow 1-litre (2-pint) baking dish. Preheat the oven to 150°C/130°C fan/Gas 2.

2 Weigh the rice into the dish, then add the sugar and pour over the milk and cream. Stir well. Grate a generous sprinkling of nutmeg on top of the mixture and dot with butter.

3 Bake for 30 minutes, stir, then bake for a further 1½ hours or until the rice has absorbed most of the milk and cream and a lovely rich skin has formed on top.

 MARY'S WISE WORDS

You must use pudding rice for this dessert as it has short starchy grains that will soak up all the milk. Omit the cream and use all milk if you want a less rich version. Serve it with a dollop of jam too, if you like.

DIPLÔME D'HONNEUR
LE CORDON BLEU

La Fondation Le Cordon Bleu garante de l'excellence culinaire dispensée dans ses Écoles Internationales, est heureuse d'attribuer ce diplôme à

Madame Mary Berry

Ancienne étudiante de l'école Le Cordon Bleu Paris - 1960

pour ses contributions et sa participation à l'essor des arts culinaires.

André J. Cointreau,
Président

A. Paris
Le 2 octobre 2012

"In times when everyone is rushed and so often watching what they eat, a fabulous homemade pudding is a rare and special treat"

QUEEN OF *Puddings*

PREPARE AHEAD
The base, custard and
meringue can be made
6 hours in advance, up
to the end of step 5.

FOR THE BASE
600ml (1 pint) full-fat milk
25g (1oz) butter, plus extra
for greasing the dish
finely grated zest of 1 lemon
50g (2oz) caster sugar
3 egg yolks
75g (3oz) fresh white
breadcrumbs
6 tablespoons blackcurrant
or strawberry jam

FOR THE MERINGUE
3 egg whites
175g (6oz) caster sugar

This old fashioned pudding is so comforting, everybody loves it and it is such an economical and easy pudding to make. If you don't have full fat milk, add a little cream to semi-skimmed.

1 Grease a 1.5-litre (2½-pint) shallow ovenproof dish (one that will fit inside a roasting tin) with butter. You will also need a plastic piping bag if you want to pipe the meringue, otherwise just spoon it on. Preheat the oven to 170°C/150°C fan/Gas 3.

2 For the base, gently warm the milk in a small pan until hand hot. Add the butter, lemon zest and sugar. Stir until dissolved. In a bowl, lightly whisk the egg yolks and then slowly add the warm milk while whisking. Keep whisking until incorporated.

3 Sprinkle the breadcrumbs over the base of the buttered dish and pour over the custard. Leave to stand for about 15 minutes, so the breadcrumbs absorb the liquid.

4 Place the dish in a roasting tin and fill the tin halfway with hot water. Bake the custard in the oven for 25–30 minutes until set. Remove from the oven and cool while you make the meringue topping. Reduce the oven temperature to 150°C/130°C fan/Gas 2.

5 To make the meringue, whisk the egg whites using an electric hand whisk on full speed until they form stiff peaks. Add the sugar a teaspoon at a time, still whisking on maximum speed until the mixture is stiff and shiny. If you want a swirly, piped top to the pudding, transfer the meringue mixture to a piping bag and snip the end to make a hole about 1cm (½ in) across.

6 Gently spread the jam on top of the custard then pipe the meringue on top of the jam or spread it on with a spoon and make little peaks so that it looks pretty. Return the pudding to the oven (not in the roasting tin) for about 25–30 minutes until the meringue is crisp and pale golden all over. Serve at once.

SAUCY *Brownie* PUD

SERVES 6

PREPARE AHEAD

Although this can be cooked
an hour or two beforehand, it
is best not to cook it the day
before as sometimes the sauce
will be absorbed into the
sponge. If you want to cook
it and then reheat it, you will
need to do so in a microwave
– the oven will dry it out.

You can also prepare the sauce
and pudding up to a few
hours in advance, but do
not pour the sauce over the
pudding until ready to bake.

150g (5oz) self-raising flour

25g (1oz) cocoa powder

125g (5oz) light
muscovado sugar

1 egg

150ml (¼ pint) milk

75g (3oz) butter,
melted and cooled

vanilla ice cream or clotted
cream, to serve

FOR THE SAUCE

75g (3oz) light
muscovado sugar

1 tablespoon cocoa powder

250ml (8fl oz) boiling water

Spoon through the sponge to discover the gooey rich sauce
underneath! This addictive pud is perfect with a good dollop
of ice cream and it's made even better by the fact that it is so
quick and easy to cook. It is best served straight from the oven
but don't worry, you can get everything ready beforehand and
assemble it just before baking.

1 Butter a shallow 1-litre (2-pint) baking dish. Preheat the oven
to 180°C/160°C fan/Gas 4.

2 Measure the flour into a mixing bowl with the cocoa powder
and sugar. Add the egg. Mix the milk and butter together then
beat into the flour mixture until smooth. Pour the mixture into
the prepared baking dish.

3 To make the sauce, mix all the ingredients together then pour
evenly over the cake mixture. Don't pour it all in one place, and
try not to disturb the sponge mixture too much.

4 Bake for 30–40 minutes, until the pudding has risen and
feels just firm to the touch. The sauce will have sunk into the
pudding and be runny underneath. Serve hot with ice cream
or clotted cream.

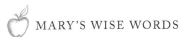 MARY'S WISE WORDS

*If you prefer, make 6 individual puddings in ramekins instead. You will
only need to bake them for 15–25 minutes.*

*Why not use hot coffee in the sauce instead of water to make a mocha pud?
Or try adding raspberries to the pudding mixture.*

WARM CHOCOLATE *Fondant* TART

SERVES 6–8

FOR THE PASTRY

100g (4oz) plain flour, plus extra for dusting

50g (2oz) icing sugar

50g (2oz) butter, diced, plus extra for greasing

1 large egg yolk

about 1 tablespoon cold water

FOR THE FILLING

100g (4oz) butter

150g (5oz) dark chocolate, no more than 60 per cent cocoa solids, finely chopped

150g (5oz) golden caster sugar

75g (3oz) plain flour

6 medium eggs

TO SERVE

a dusting of icing sugar

a few small strawberries, to decorate (optional)

pouring cream (optional)

This tart looks like something you might have bought from a French patisserie, but it is so easy to make. I like it served gently warmed (see page 268) with a dusting of icing sugar, but you could make it really glamorous by topping it with chocolate curls, a drizzle of melted chocolate or a little whipped cream and fresh summer berries.

1 Butter a 23cm (9in) fluted flan tin. To make the pastry, measure the flour and icing sugar into a large bowl and rub in the butter with your fingertips until the mixture resembles fine breadcrumbs (this can also be done in a food processor). Add the egg yolk and water and mix until it comes together to form a firm dough. Wrap in clingfilm and leave to rest in the fridge for about 30 minutes.

2 Preheat the oven to 200°C/180°C fan/Gas 6. Dust the work surface with flour then roll out the pastry as thinly as you can to a circle about 5cm larger than your flan tin. Line the tin with the pastry. Don't worry if the pastry breaks a little, it is easy to patch up. Chill for 15 minutes.

3 Prick the base of the pastry with a fork, line the pastry case with baking paper or foil and fill with baking beans. Bake the pastry blind for 10 minutes, until just lightly golden, then remove the paper and beans and return the tart to the oven to cook for a further 5–7 minutes until pale golden and the base is cooked.

Continues overleaf

This tart can be made 1–2 days in advance. Bring it to room temperature and warm it slightly in a low oven (120°C/100°C fan/Gas ½) for 10 minutes. You can also make and bake the pastry case blind up to a week in advance (store it in a cake tin), then add the filling and bake half an hour before serving.

FREEZE

The tart can be baked and frozen for up to 1 month. Defrost completely then warm through in a low oven (120°C/100°C fan/Gas ½) for 10 minutes.

4 To make the filling, melt the butter in a medium pan over a low heat, then add the chocolate and stir until melted and smooth. Remove from the heat and stir in the sugar and flour. Whisk in the eggs one at a time.

5 Place the flan tin on a baking tray. Pour the mixture into the pastry case, filling it right to the top, and place in the oven. (If you have any mixture left over, cook it in a ramekin for 5 minutes and enjoy as a cook's treat!) Bake the tart for 10–12 minutes until just set around the edges but still slightly wobbly in the centre.

6 Remove from the oven and allow to cool slightly, until warm not piping hot. Dust with icing sugar. If liked cut a shape out of baking paper and place on top of the tart before dusting with icing sugar, then remove the paper to make a stencilled effect. Or serve the tart warm with strawberries and cream.

 MARY'S WISE WORDS

If you don't have time to rest the pastry in the fridge for 30 minutes you can roll it out, line the tin and freeze it for 10 minutes before baking blind.

Use a good-quality bar of chocolate with a high percentage of cocoa solids (40–60 per cent) for a rich flavour.

You can also make this as 8 individual tartlets baked in bun tins. Cook for about 4 minutes, making sure the mixture still has a wobble in the centre.

RHUBARB AND *Orange* COBBLER

SERVES 6

PREPARE AHEAD

This is best made and served as soon as it is baked, but any leftovers can be kept in the fridge for up to 2 days.

800g (1lb 12oz) early rhubarb, trimmed and cut into 5cm (2in) lengths

150g (5oz) caster sugar

grated zest and juice of 2 oranges

cream or custard, to serve

FOR THE SCONE COBBLER

150g (5oz) self-raising flour

½ teaspoon baking powder

75g (3oz) caster sugar

50g (2oz) softened butter

75ml (2½fl oz) milk

about 2 tablespoons demerara sugar

Cobblers can be sweet or savoury but as a dessert, they are essentially a stewed-fruit filling topped with a crust made from a scone-like dough. The topping in this recipe is rolled out fairly thinly making it less robust than a traditional cobbler might be, and there is a generous amount of rhubarb.

1 You will need a 1.5-litre (3-pint) baking dish and a 5cm (2in) pastry cutter. Preheat the oven to 180°C/160°C fan/Gas 4.

2 Arrange the rhubarb in the baking dish, add the caster sugar, half the orange zest and all the orange juice.

3 Measure the flour, baking powder and caster sugar into a mixing bowl. Add the butter and rub it into the flour until the mixture resembles breadcrumbs. Stir in the milk and remaining orange zest and mix to a soft dough. Turn the dough on to a lightly floured work surface and pat out until about 1cm (½in) thick. Cut into circles using the cutter. Arrange the scones on top of the rhubarb in a circle around the edge of the dish then sprinkle with the demerara sugar.

4 Bake for 30–40 minutes until the rhubarb is tender when tested with the point of a knife and the cobbler is golden brown. Serve hot with cream or custard.

 MARY'S WISE WORDS *Make this cobbler with any seasonal fruits; try apples and blackberries, plums or summer berries.*

PLUM AND *Marzipan* TARTE TATIN

SERVES 8

75g (3oz) light
  muscovado sugar

about 7–9 large firm
  plums, roughly 500g
  (1lb 2oz) in total, halved,
  stones removed

100g (4oz) marzipan

1 x 320g pack ready-rolled
  all-butter puff pastry

This is a cheat's variation of the classic French tart and makes an impressive pudding to serve with lots of cream, ice cream or crème fraîche.

1 You will need a 23cm (9in) round, fixed-base cake tin, at least 5cm (2in) deep. Preheat the oven to 220°C/200°C fan/Gas 7.

2 Sprinkle the sugar over the base of the tin in an even layer. Arrange the plums on top of the sugar, cut-side down.

3 Roll out the marzipan to a round slightly smaller than the tin and place on top of the plums.

4 Roll out the pastry just a little bit bigger so that it is the width of the cake tin. Place the cake tin on top of the pastry. Using the tin as a guide, cut around the tin to make a circle, then lay the pastry over the plums and tuck the edges of the pastry down around the fruit. Make a small cross in the top of the pastry to let the steam escape during baking.

5 Bake for 25–30 minutes until the pastry is crisp and golden and the plums are tender. Loosen the edges of the tarte then turn out on to a plate and serve.

 MARY'S WISE WORDS

If you have small plums, you might need to use a few more to cover the tarte.

If your plums are very ripe you will get lots more juice, so tip the juices into a pan and boil rapidly, before pouring over the turned out tarte.

Don't be tempted to use a loose-bottomed cake tin or a springform tin or you will lose all the juices. It is a good idea to bake the tarte on a baking tray in case the juices bubble over the top of the tin.

Afternoon Tea

AFTERNOON TEA

Sitting down to a homemade tea is a real treat, and such a lovely way to entertain friends. I enjoy getting out my mother's teacups and teapot and serving a proper tea with carefully cut sandwiches and a selection of cakes and scones. It may seem simple, but I do hope my tips are helpful when you come to prepare sandwiches for your own large gatherings (pages 276–279).

I am never without a tin of shortbread to offer visitors, but I wanted to give you a new twist on the classic version so have added cranberries and white chocolate chips to the dough (page 306). The resulting biscuits are irresistible – I often have to hide the tin from myself.

Many people like to bake cakes for charity sales and school fetes, so there are some delicious tray bakes that will fly off the cake stall. Try the Chocolate and Ginger Flapjacks (page 297) or the Sultana and Cranberry Tray Bake (page 291). My Rich Chocolate Tray Bake (page 294) is a real winner too – a lovely moist sponge with a milk chocolate ganache icing.

I am always so delighted to receive the letters telling me that I have inspired you to bake, particularly from young children (many of whom seem to know more about baking than their parents now!) so I couldn't do a book without including some of my classic bakes, such as scones (page 301) and butterfly cakes (page 280). There are two variations on a sponge cake too, one with marzipan grated through it (page 287) and the other layered with lots of lemon mascarpone icing (page 282). These have become some of my new favourites – I hope you will like them too.

Teatime SANDWICHES

**MAKES 24
SANDWICHES
(TO SERVE 6)**

12 slices of bread from
a thin-cut white or
  brown loaf

butter

fillings of your choice
  (see page 279)

No afternoon tea would be complete without a selection of little sandwiches, and over the years I have discovered how to make large platters of sandwiches that can be prepared ahead without compromising on freshness or flavour. Here are my top tips for making the perfect, dainty sandwiches, along with my favourite fillings (see page 279).

1 Butter all the slices of bread on one side, top half the slices with the filling(s) of your choice and sandwich together. Leave the crusts on.

2 Arrange the sandwiches in piles of four on a large tray (check first that it will fit in your fridge). Cover with a layer of damp kitchen paper, then cover tightly with clingfilm and place the tray in the fridge.

3 Two hours before serving, slice off the crusts and cut the sandwiches into fingers or if you prefer, quarters – either triangles or squares. Cover with cling film and keep at room temperature until ready to serve. They will taste as fresh as the moment you made them.

 MARY'S WISE WORDS *Tomatoes and cucumber will make sandwiches go soggy so should only be used in sandwiches made on the day. It is best to remove their seeds too. Cut cucumber in half and scoop out the seeds with a teaspoon. Cut tomatoes in half and scoop out the seeds with your fingers.*

BLACKBERRY *Friands*

MAKES 20 FRIANDS

PREPARE AHEAD
The baked cakes will keep
in the fridge for 2 days.

FREEZE
Freeze for up to 3 months.
Defrost at room temperature
– they will only take a couple
of hours to defrost.

200g (7oz) unsalted butter,
plus extra for greasing
225g (8oz) icing sugar
75g (3oz) plain flour
150g (5oz) ground almonds
½ teaspoon almond extract
6 egg whites
150g (6oz) fresh blackberries
25g (1oz) flaked almonds
icing sugar, to dust

Friands are deliciously moist, light and buttery cakes. They are
not over-sweet, so are ideal for afternoon tea. Made from ground
almonds and butter, they use egg whites to lighten the mixture so
there is no need for a raising agent. They are traditionally cooked
in oval or barquette tins, but I just bake them in a non-stick
muffin tray without any paper cases (see Mary's Wise Words).

1 Grease one or two non-stick or silicone muffin tray(s). Preheat
the oven to 200°C/180°C fan/Gas 6.

2 Melt the butter in a small pan then remove from the heat and
leave to cool a little.

3 Sift the icing sugar and flour into a bowl and stir in the ground
almonds and extract.

4 Whisk the egg whites in a clean, grease-free bowl until they are
foamy – they do not need to have soft peaks. Add the egg whites
and melted butter to the dry ingredients and using a large metal
spoon fold the mixture together until just combined.

5 Divide the mixture between the muffin tin(s). The mixture
should come to about three quarters of the way up each hole.
Add two or three blackberries to each one and sprinkle with a
few flaked almonds. Bake for 15–20 minutes until firm in the
centre. Leave to cool for 5 minutes then turn out on to a wire
rack to cool. Dust with icing sugar before serving.

 MARY'S WISE WORDS

*Don't worry if you only have one muffin tin, bake the first batch, then cook the
remainder later. Or use a mini muffin tin or a bun tin as well. They will take
a little less time to cook, about 10–12 minutes.*

*Cultivated blackberries can be very large, so cut them in half if necessary.
You could also use raspberries too.*

CRANBERRY AND WHITE CHOCOLATE *Shortbread*

MAKES 8 WEDGES

PREPARE AHEAD
This will keep in a cake
  tin for up to 1 week.

FREEZE
This will keep for 2 months
  in the freezer. Defrost at
  room temperature.

100g (4oz) plain flour,
  plus extra for dusting

50g (2oz) semolina

100g (4oz) softened butter,
  plus extra for greasing

50g (2oz) caster sugar,
  plus extra to finish

50g (2oz) dried cranberries

50g (2oz) white
  chocolate chips

I always have a tin of shortbread ready to offer friends (and always keep a stock in the freezer too). For me, the addition of cranberries and white chocolate chips has made this shortbread even more irresistible. Use dark chocolate chips if you prefer.

1 Preheat the oven to 150°C/130°C fan/Gas 2. Lightly butter a baking tray.

2 Mix the flour and semolina together in a bowl, add the butter and rub in with your fingertips until the mixture resembles breadcrumbs. Stir in the sugar, cranberries and chocolate chips. Squeeze the mixture together to make a smooth dough.

3 Roll out the dough on a lightly floured work surface into a 20cm (8in) round. Lift on to the baking tray. Crimp the edges to decorate. Prick all over with a fork and score into 8 wedges with a sharp knife. Chill for about 30 minutes until firm.

4 Bake for 40 minutes or until pale golden. Mark the wedges again and sprinkle the shortbread with caster sugar.

5 Allow the shortbread to cool on the baking tray for 5 minutes, then lift off carefully and transfer to a wire rack to cool completely. Cut into wedges to serve.

 MARY'S WISE WORDS *Semolina gives the shortbread a lovely crunch but you can use cornflour or rice flour instead. You will find dried cranberries in all the supermarkets.*

AFTERNOON TEA

Teatime Scones

*Whole Lemon Cake with
Lemon Cheesecake Icing*

*Chocolate Tray Bake with
Feathered Icing*

*Apple and Cinnamon
Loaf Cake*

Teatime Sandwiches

Orange Butterfly Cakes

INDEX

stew, rich beef and mushroom 102–4
Stilton butter 108–9
stir-fried vegetables, with
  Asian belly of pork 144–6
strawberry
  freeze-dried 29
  jam 308
  rosé wine jellies with
    summer fruits 232–3
sugar 29–30
sugar paste 34
sultana
  cinnamon and sultana scones 302
  and cranberry tray bake 291
summer pudding loaf 234–6
sunflower seeds: apple crumble with
  walnut and sunflower seeds 258–9
Sussex pond pudding with
  apple 254–7
sweet potato 178–9
sweetcorn 127

T
tahini 28
tarragon 24
  peppered tarragon chicken 122–3
tart, warm chocolate fondant 266–8
tarte tatin, plum and marzipan 270
tartlets
  blue cheese and fig filo
    tartlets 58–9
  tiny pesto tartlets 57
terrine, salmon and asparagus 76–8
Thai-spiced tomato soup 90–1
thyme 24
toasts, croque Monsieur 45
tomato 17
  avocado, tomato and mint
    salad 86–7
  cheese, tomato and thyme
    scones 302
  cherry tomato and
    mozzarella salad 96
  cobb salad with ranch-style
    dressing 166–7
  crab cocktail 70–1
  fresh tomato relish 111–12
  and goat's cheese canapés 46–8
  and onion galettes 82–3
  passata 17

pastitsio 132
purée 17
sauce 128–31
sun-blushed 17
sun-dried 17
Thai-spiced tomato soup 90–1
triple tomato risotto 113
vegetable casserole 134–5
tray bakes
  rich chocolate tray bake with
    feathered icing 294–6
  sultana and cranberry
    tray bake 291
trifle
  summer glory trifle cake 246–8
  mango and passion fruit trifle 249
tuna
  Asian tuna skewers 50–1
  canapés 37
  Hobie's tuna pasta bake 127

V
vanilla 30
vegetable(s)
  Asian belly of pork with
    stir-fried vegetables 144–6
  freezing 33
  roasted vegetables 95
  salmon en croûte with
    pesto-roasted vegetables 150–3
  spiced garden vegetable
    casserole 134–5
  vegetable platter 178–9
  see also specific vegetables
vegetarian recipes
  asparagus mousse 69
  avocado, tomato and
    mint salad 86–7
  blue cheese and fig filo
    tartlets 58–9
  broad bean and little gem
    salad 198–9
  butternut squash and
    spinach lasagne 128–31
  creamy celeriac soup 89
  crunchy broccoli salad 213
  fiery red rice and carrot
    salad 208–9
  foolproof green salad with
    dill dressing 202

fresh tomato relish 111–12
garlic mushroom bruschetta 88
goat's cheese, pomegranate and
  onion salad with balsamic
  dressing 212
goat's cheese and tomato
  canapés 46–8
jewelled couscous salad 210–11
lime coleslaw 213
mustard mash 105
pistachio basil pesto with
  fettuccine 162–3
quail's egg croustades with spinach
  and Hollandaise sauce 60–1
raita 111–12
roasted fennel, onion and potato,
  with Parmesan topping 206–7
sharing platter 92–6
spiced garden vegetable
  casserole 134–5
spinach, gruyère and ham
  quiche 124–6
Thai-spiced tomato soup 90–1
tiny pesto tartlets 57
tomato and onion galettes 82–3
triple tomato risotto 113
the ultimate roast potato 176–7
vegetable platter 178–9
Yorkshire pudding 182
venison and chestnut pie 140–3
vinegar 20–1

W
walnuts: apple crumble with walnuts
  and sunflower seeds 258–9
watercress
  foolproof green salad with
    dill dressing 202
  scallops with lemon and dill
    sauce and watercress 66–7
white chocolate
  cranberry and white chocolate
    shortbread 306–7
  rich chocolate tray bake with
    feathered icing 294–6
wine
  rosé wine jellies with
    summer fruits 232–3

Y
yoghurt 111–12, 231, 244–5, 249, 309
Yorkshire pudding 182

ACKNOWLEDGEMENTS

Life has never been busier and I am loving every minute of it! But I couldn't do it without the help of my best friend and assistant of over 24 years, Lucy Young, and cookery assistant Lucinda Kaizik. I am so lucky to have them and could not do what I do without them.

For this book we were also joined by home economist Mitzie Wilson, she is immensely talented and has a wealth of experience to share. She and Lucinda have been cooking up all the recipes each week – we have had some very fun lunches together and indulged in many delicious meals from this book, so you can be assured that everything has been thoroughly tried and tested! And of course, my husband Paul, my children, their other halves and my grandchildren have all helped out with tastings and suggestions too.

Thank you to the brilliant photographer Georgia Glynn Smith for her stunning work – what a delight to work with, such fun and an amazing eye for the different shot! Kim Morphew has again excelled as home economist, creating our recipes with care and passion, what a team. Thanks too to Kate Fox and Muna Reyal at BBC Books, alongside Lucy Stephens, Imogen Fortes and Polly Webb-Wilson for their work on putting the book together.

We have had an amazing film crew filming the TV series which goes with this book from our home and on location. Headed by Richard Bowron, Scott Tankard and Sophie Lloyd and wonderful home economists Lisa Harrison and Georgia May, plus of course Tom, Rik and Tim the camera guys who kept me smiling.

As you can see, we have had some wonderful parties while making this book – I hope you do while using it too!

Mary Berry